LET
THIS
Mind
BE IN
YOU

LET THIS Mind BE IN YOU

FRANCES HUNTER

Whitaker House

LET THIS MIND BE IN YOU:
Thinking the Thoughts of Jesus

Frances Hunter
Hunter Ministries
P.O. Box 5600
Kingwood, TX 77325-5600
www.cfhunter.org
e-mail: wec@cfhunter.org

ISBN: 0-88368-626-0
Printed in the United States of America
© 2000 by Frances Hunter

Whitaker House
30 Hunt Valley Circle
New Kensington, PA 15068
www.whitakerhouse.com

Library of Congress Cataloging-in-Publication Data

Hunter, Frances Gardner, 1916–
Let this mind be in you : thinking the thoughts of Jesus / by Frances Hunter.
p.   cm.
ISBN 0-88368-626-0 (alk. paper)
1. Christian life. I. Title.
BV4501.2 .H828   2000
248.4dc21   00-009595

2 3 4 5 6 7 8 9 10 11 12 **ய** 12 11 10 09 08 07 06 05 04

Contents

Let this mind be in you which was also in Christ Jesus.
—Philippians 2:5

One

Say "Yes" to Jesus

———————●———————

The magnitude of God's love for us and what He does for us at the very moment of our spiritual conception when we are born again by the Spirit of God is one of the most awe-inspiring miracles in the world!

When we sincerely receive the revelation of what we actually acquire as a born-again child of God, it takes us into a supernatural realm that is so far beyond our human ability to understand that we should all fall on our faces and worship God the Father.

To me, one of the most exciting realms into which God takes us is described in 1 Corinthians 2:16 concerning the fact that we actually possess the mind of Christ. I especially love the way it is expressed in the *Amplified Bible, "But we have the mind of Christ, the Messiah, and do hold the thoughts (feelings and purposes) of His heart."*

God loves us so much that He is willing to take our dirty, sinful minds (remember those dirty jokes you used to tell and dirty thoughts you used to think) and replace them with the actual mind of Christ so that we have His thoughts, His feelings, His attitudes, and His purposes instilled and placed into what was formerly our old nature. (See 2 Corinthians 5:17.) What kind of a God is this that He can love us that much?

Philippians 2:5 says, *"Let this mind be in you which was also in Christ Jesus."* The very thought that God would let the mind of Christ be in us is so supernatural that it is impossible for the natural mind to understand; however, the thing that is so totally and completely exciting about this is what happens to our lives as we begin to realize and actually allow this mind to be in us, *"which was also in Christ Jesus."*

Consider these three questions:

- How should we think?

- How should we act?

- How should we behave?

How can we know the answers to all these questions? It is so easy if we just understand the principles of possessing the mind of Christ.

Throughout his lifetime, Paul taught about the mystery of the ages, which was, *"Christ in you, the hope of glory"* (Col. 1:27). Many people cannot grasp the promise that when we are born again by the Spirit of God, Jesus Christ comes to live His life *in* and *through* us. We actually have the Spirit of Christ, His ability, and His power locked up within us when we are born again by the Spirit of God.

When I think that we have the actual mind of Christ, it is difficult for me to even stay on this earth. I feel like I could go into orbit and never come back again when I realize that God has placed in our hands such a priceless possession as the very mind of Christ.

The questions asked of us more than any other are, "How can I know the will of God?" "What am I supposed to do as a Christian?" "How am I supposed to act?"

It is so easy to find out! All you have to do is to open the Bible!

Pick up a red-letter edition of the Bible. Each time you see the red letters, you know that is what Jesus said. If we believe and say the words that Jesus said and then act upon them, we will be operating with the mind of Christ.

Many people have a possession, but never enjoy it, never use it, and never get anything out of it. This is what happens to far too many people concerning the invaluable possession of the actual mind of Christ.

We may have the priceless opportunity to possess it, but we can never really possess it until we are willing to totally and completely submerge our own personalities, wills, and intellects into the mind of Christ and let Him begin to operate in and through us. The day that the body of Christ learns to do this is going to be the day when the wraps will be taken off the power of God! The Devil will know he has to run, and the body of Christ will finally understand fully that the Devil has to run. Because we possess the very mind of Christ, we have all power in heaven and in earth!

Any of the Gospels in the New Testament will start you on the road to discovering how to react under all circumstances, simply because we have allowed this mind to be in us, *"which was also in Christ Jesus."*

In Luke 4:4 we read, *"It is written, 'Man shall not live by bread alone, but by every word of God.'"*

If we are going to operate with the mind of Christ, if we are going to literally possess the mind of Christ, then we are going to have to believe what this verse says. We are not going to live by physical food alone, but we are going to live by spiritual food, which is the Word of God. If we are going to live by every word of God, then we certainly need to know what the Word of God says. Only then can we sit ourselves down to a beautiful and exciting feast all the time. God places His Spirit in us when we receive the gift of the Holy Spirit. Therein lies our source of power to give life to the Word.

The Word of God, or the Word that God speaks, is alive and full of power, making it active, operative, energizing, and effective. Do you realize that if we live by the Word of God, we will be full of power? We will be operative! We will be energized. We will be able to be alive in Christ and be effective at all times. There is no physical food that will give you the same type of energy, power, wisdom, and discernment as the Word of God.

Why is the Word of God so powerful? Because our all-powerful God is the One who spoke the Word, and He personally backs what He says.

There have been many times when I have been so exhausted I felt I could not go on—times when my body has cried out for sleep and rest. Instead, I have gone into the Word of God and come out of the pages an actual tiger with no lack of energy! Nothing will inject energy and power into your mind and body like God's Word! So, if we are going to live and breathe and be energized and empowered by every word of God, then we certainly need to know what the Word of God says.

Let us go to the eighth verse in that same chapter of Luke's gospel. It reads, *"And Jesus answered and said to him, 'Get behind Me, Satan! For it is written, "You shall worship the Lord your God, and Him only you shall serve."'"* If we have the mind of Christ, what are we going to be doing? We are going to worship the Lord. We will not worship anything else.

We are not going to worship television!

We are not going to worship movies!

We are not going to worship homes!

We are not going to worship fancy clothes!

We are not going to worship undesirable habits and attitudes—which actually is worshipping only ourselves. This is a form of idolatry.

We are going to worship the Lord.

There are many people who worship a television set. They will sit in front of it and worship it for hours. They will sit and watch soap operas hour after hour, knowing full well that there is nothing spiritual, nothing to be gained, nothing that will uplift them, and nothing that will edify them as they watch the humdrum TV programs day after day.

If we are going to truly operate with the mind of Christ, then we are going to do exactly what Jesus did. We are going to worship the Lord and nothing else! All of these things become obsolete when we really put Jesus first in our lives. Suddenly, "the things of this world will grow strangely dim in the light of His glory and grace" if we really keep our eyes on Jesus. Therefore, because we have the mind of Christ, we are not going to worship the things of the world.

We are not going to worship golf games on Sunday instead of going to church.

We are not going to worship fishing and boating; we are not going to worship guns or trophies!

We are not going to worship vacations over serving God!

We are not going to worship entertainment, country clubs, or other worldly things over the things of God. *"Do not love the world or the things in the world. If anyone loves the world, the love of the Father is not in him"* (1 John 2:15).

When we let the mind of Christ actually possess us, and when we possess the mind of Christ, our minds will be thinking in exactly the same direction as Jesus. Our answers will be the same as His, and our dedicated, daily lives will be the same as His. We will be out there doing exactly the same things Jesus did!

Here is something that is going to "get" a lot of people. That's why I decided to put this point in at the very beginning of this book. One of the most difficult areas for many individuals to use the mind of Christ is the area of finances. We do not have difficulty wanting to believe to receive from God. We have problems in giving to God.

This area is so important in my life because God dealt with me within seconds after I had been born again. I had not even been saved a split second when the almighty God spoke to me. His words changed my entire thinking about giving.

I had always been a real tightwad where giving to God was concerned. I never went to church without checking first to see that I had a single one dollar bill in my wallet. There wasn't a preacher in the world who was going to get more than a dollar out of me. It would have never entered my mind to give a five dollar bill, a ten, or a twenty. Twenty dollars would have meant that I was a spendthrift!

God always knows exactly how to deal with us on the level where we are. I had not even been saved more than two seconds when God spoke to me.

There was no doubt in my mind it was God. I had gone from sinner to saint in less than two seconds. God was already speaking to me! I was overjoyed!

The God who made the universe had taken time out to speak to me, and the words He said were the sweetest music to my ears that I had ever heard because *He* said them! "I want twenty percent of everything you've got!" I thought that was His charge for saving me. I was so ignorant of the Bible that I didn't know my salvation was free.

The important thing was that I knew it was the voice of God, and I didn't have to wait until three or four people confirmed it. I heard God and didn't question it. I didn't wonder for a single minute if it was the Devil or one of his cohorts. I knew instantly it was God! He didn't yell or holler or threaten me with dire disaster if I disobeyed. He simply gave me an opportunity to be an obedient new baby.

I would never have considered disobeying God. All I knew was that I had heard God and I wanted to obey Him. From the moment of salvation, all I have ever wanted to do was obey God.

Let's take a look and see what caused this tremendous turnaround in my giving pattern. Because I was truly born again, I became a *"new creature"* (2 Cor. 5:17 KJV) in Christ, so I instantly acquired the mind of Christ. My thinking patterns changed immediately. I didn't have to work on them; they just changed because I was a new creation. My mind would never have let me argue with God over whether or not to be obedient. Jesus never argued with His Father. When we truly are born again and let His mind be in us, then it will be easy for us to hear and heed that *"still small voice"* (1 Kings 19:12) of God.

We possess the mind of Christ. Therefore, we think exactly the same way Jesus does when it comes to giving.

What does Jesus think about giving?

Does He think we should *hoard* our money?

Does He think we should *stockpile* our money?

Does He think we should *hide* it?

Does He think we should *save* it for a rainy day?

Let us take a look at Scripture and see what it says:

> **Give,** *and it will be given to you: good measure, pressed down, shaken together, and running over will be put into your bosom. For with the same measure that you use, it will be measured back to you.* (Luke 6:38, emphasis added)

Many people think when an offering is taken that this is a very tacky time; this is a time when we need to count our pennies; this is a time when we need to see if we have enough money left to pay all of our bills.

Is this what Jesus said? Does He say hide it, stash it, store it away? No, Jesus has other things to say. He says, *"Give, and it will be given to you"* (emphasis added). Many people don't believe in the giving and receiving system or the sowing and the reaping system. If we possess the mind of Christ, what else can we believe? We must believe exactly the same as He does because He promised in His Word that if we give, we are definitely going to have our needs met—*"exceedingly abundantly"* (Eph. 3:20) met—more than we can dream or imagine.

Someone said to me one time, "Don't you think that is really presumptuous to give and expect God to give back to you?"

I said, "No, for the very simple reason that when I prayed the sinner's prayer and asked God to save me, I expected God to fulfill His Word." The one thing that God is obligated to do, and wants to do, is to fulfill His Word.

When I gave Him my sins, He gave me forgiveness. When I confessed with my mouth that Jesus Christ was Lord, He came into my heart and saved me.

I expected Him to do this because He promises it! Therefore, when I give, I anticipate that God will give it back because He said so in His Word! Because we have allowed the mind of Christ to be in us, we need to anticipate that when we give, when we tithe, and when we make separate offerings over and beyond the tithe, these offerings are going to come back. There is a money-back guarantee that is signed in the New Testament by the Son of the Living God, Jesus, who says when you give, you are going to get it back.

He doesn't promise a possibility; He promises a reality! Besides our being blessed by His return system, God is blessed even more because He receives back our willingness to trust Him as our investment advisor.

Allowing the mind of Christ to be in us means that we have no doubt in this area. It doesn't say, "Well, I think God will do it for somebody else, but He won't do it for me. Because the mind of Christ is in me, I know that I know that I know that Jesus is going to return it to me."

He may not always return it to me when I think it should be returned, but because I possess the mind of Christ, I know that I know that I know that it is coming back to me. I am not going to change my thinking that would cause me to disagree with Jesus. My thinking is going to line up with His! Jesus knows our hearts and knows whether we selfishly want more for ourselves or whether we want more for the kingdom of God.

One of the greatest desires of my heart is to get the message across to the body of Christ about giving to God. I know what it did in my own life when I learned to give, because until God gets your money, He never gets you! I use Luke 6:38 over and over again as I take offerings so that Christians will believe that when they give, they will receive it back.

Every once in a while I say to myself, "God, people never get the message of what I'm talking about." I keep preaching on giving to God and wonder occasionally if anybody really hears what I have to say about giving.

A Child Can Understand

As we were eating in our local cafeteria one day, a pastor and his family were eating there, too. As a way of saying hello, I leaned over their table and said, "I came over to get a bite of your food because I didn't have enough." The pastor's eight-year-old son picked up his chocolate pie and gave it to me. I said, "Honey, I wouldn't take your pie. I was only kidding."

He said, "Go ahead and take it, because if you take it, I'll get back a lot more than what is on that plate right now!"

He got the message! He got the message that when you give, it is going to *"be given* [back] *to you: good measure, pressed down, shaken together, and running* [all] *over"* (Luke 6:38) the place. I said, "Glory to God!" and you could have heard me all over the cafeteria. If no one else sitting under my ministry when I take an offering ever listened and believed what I said, I found one who did. An eight-year-old boy!

We need to believe so fervently that, like the eight-year-old boy, we will be willing to give up the most special part of our dinner, knowing that Jesus always gives back more! (And He did. The Lord directed me to take an offering for that little boy at the next church service. It amounted to more than $200!)

It is exciting to be a Christian and to recognize what we really do possess because we operate with the mind of Christ. Luke 8:16 reads, *"No one, when he has lit a lamp, covers it with a vessel or puts it under a bed, but sets it on a lampstand, that those who enter may see the light."*

Christians ought to be the most brilliant lights in the world and the loudest blabbermouths in the world. We are going to do exactly what Jesus does because we have His very mind.

We are not going to hide our little light. We are not going to put our heads underneath a bushel basket and just hide ourselves away. Because we are like Jesus Christ, we are going to hold our candles up high for the whole world to see! We are going to talk about Jesus wherever we are. We are going to talk about Jesus in airports. We are going to talk about Jesus in the grocery store. We are going to talk about Jesus at the service station.

If we allow His mind to be in us, we are going to be filled with that overwhelming, bubbling desire to see that the whole world gets saved. We are not going to let our lights go out! We are going to let them shine brighter and brighter and brighter all the time!

Charles and I have the most marvelous time in the world wherever we go. If it is in an airport, we are singing. Many times we sing in tongues. Many times we just go through airports praising God and having an exciting time. Often people walk up to me and say, "Are you a bride?" just because we look so happy. What a wonderful opportunity this gives us to witness. I say, "Yes, we are the bride of Christ," and we share Jesus with them.

Jesus never hid His light under a bushel. He let His light shine all the time; and as Christians who possess the mind of Christ, we should all do exactly the same thing.

Think of the glory that is going to come to the Father when we all do this. Think how His heart will leap with joy when people begin to look at us and know there is something real superspecial about us!

> *Then He said to them all, "If anyone desires to come after Me, let him deny himself, and take up his cross daily, and follow Me. For whoever desires to save his life will lose it, but whoever loses his life for My sake will save it."* (Luke 9:23–24)

Many people say, "Well, my cross is my unsaved husband, that drunken alcoholic. He has been the cross I have carried all these years. He has been an albatross around my neck. He has weighed me down all of these years. He is the cross that I must bear. Because I bear it, I am going to make it into heaven someday."

Some people say, "Oh, the cross I have to bear is this sickness God gave me. Paul had a thorn in the flesh, and God never healed him. (See 2 Corinthians 12:7–10.) The cross I am bearing is this sickness that I have that I will never get over. But I will glorify God, because I will continue to love Him in spite of all this."

Beloved, that is not what Jesus is talking about. If we allow His mind to be in us, we are going to think exactly the same way He did!

Alive to God, Dead to Self

Why did Jesus carry His cross? Because it was something that God had saddled Him with? No, Jesus carried His cross so that He could die willingly to save us. He could have called *"legions of angels"* (Matt. 26:53) to rescue Him. He chose to suffer and die because He knew the victory that He could then share with you and me.

When we pick up our cross daily, it is to die to self so that our ambitions, our desires, our wants, our longings, and our unquenchable thirst for the lusts and pleasures of this world will be crucified every day.

Remember what Paul said:

I have been crucified with Christ; it is no longer I who live, but Christ lives in me; and the life which I now live in the flesh I live by faith in the Son of God, who loved me and gave Himself for me. (Gal. 2:20)

Jesus carried His cross to die for us; we need to carry our cross to die for Him.

This death is a spiritual dying to self every day so that all of these worldly appetites that come up are trodden down. That is the real cross that we bear!

The cross you have to bear is not that unsaved husband. It is not that unsaved wife. It is not those unsaved children who are out there in the world. The cross you need to bear is the cross of dying every day to self and earthly desires.

I was talking to a girl the other night, and she asked me to pray that people would stop hurting her feelings. She said, "People are so mean to me, and I get my feelings hurt all of the time."

I said, "No, I am not going to pray for you." She was startled, so I went on to explain: "What you need to do is to die to self so that people cannot hurt your feelings. Did you ever see a dead man get out of a casket and say to the pastor, 'You hurt my feelings because of what you just said about me?'"

Remember if you are dead to self, you cannot have your feelings hurt. People cannot hurt you by the things they say about you. God's Word tells us that we can expect to be persecuted by people who have the carnal mind, because *"the carnal mind is enmity against God"* (Rom. 8:7). We need to die to self every day if we really have allowed the mind of Christ to be in us! We must remember to keep all of these worldly things out of our minds and hearts at all times. Then we need to follow Jesus, which means to do the same things He did on this earth, because He says whoever wishes to save his own life will lose it (Luke 9:24). In other words, if you keep worrying about saving your own life and doing your own thing, you will lose it all. But if you lose your life for Jesus' sake, you will save it. Save what? Your very life! Your eternal life!

Use What You Own

You can have something and never really possess it! Years ago every girl had to have a hope chest before she got married.

There were always three things she had to buy first of all. She might have been so poor that she didn't own a pair of decent shoes, but no self-respecting girl who expected to get married could ever get past eighteen years of age and fail to start a set of china, silverware, and crystal.

I started to work at the very height of the depression. Salaries were unbelievably low. I know what it means not to have anything at all, but one of the first things I did after I started working was to buy one piece of china. It took me seven months to pay for it. Then I bought one piece of crystal. It took a year to pay for that! Then came one silver teaspoon. I don't think I ever finished paying for that!

Many girls did go on to fill out the entire set of china, crystal, and silverware, but because all of these things were so expensive and it had taken so long to pay for them, they were all carefully put away and never used. Those special treasures were taken out and used only at Christmas, Thanksgiving, and Easter. Except to eat from them very carefully, no one except Mother could touch them or wash them. The china and crystal were so delicate that there was always fear they might break or the silver would get lost, so all of these expensive items were never used. They sat in breakfronts and china cabinets to be shown off to everyone who came to visit, but to enjoy by using them—never!

You can have the most beautiful china in the world, but it doesn't do you a bit of good if you don't use it. You can have the most delicate crystal and the most ornate silverware. It doesn't do you a bit of good if you don't use it. You own it, yes, but you don't really possess it.

I enjoy everything I own. I use my crystal. I use my china. I use my silver. If something gets broken, first I ask,

"Did anybody get hurt?" If everybody is okay, I say, "Hallelujah!" All those worldly things can be replaced.

Because I possess everything I own, I enjoy everything to the utmost. I do not save things for a later date. I buy a new dress and wear it the next day. I use everything I possess, and I possess everything I own.

Let's apply this principle to the mind of Christ. We should not take what we are given at that moment when we are born again and put it up on a shelf and say, "Now, as soon as I get over all of these problems, I am going to take the mind of Christ off the shelf and stick it in my head. Then I'll begin to use what was given to me when I was born again."

Many people say, "I am really going to be a committed Christian as soon as I clean up the mess in my life." Become a committed Christian first; then the mess in your life will get cleaned up without your exerting a lot of effort! Realizing that we possess the mind of Christ and making sure in our spirits that we know that we know that we know that the thinking mechanism we have is actually the mind of Christ will take us into supernatural realms and out of the realm of the unsaved world.

What Are You Eating?

The world says "You are what you eat." Let's apply that statement to our Christian lives. What you eat in the natural will either nourish you or harm you. The same is true with the spiritual food you eat. You eat of the Bible and grow upon God's laws, or you eat the messages of the world and turn your back on God.

The principles that are listed in the Word of God are extremely important. The Word of God tells you how to operate in today's world.

Jesus said, *"It is written, 'Man shall not live by bread alone, but by every word of God'"* (Luke 4:4).

This doesn't say that you will live by only the portions of Scripture that you like or that tickle your fancy. Some portions may be a little hard to listen to because they apply to you and may hit a little close to home.

We need to be nourished by the Word of God and not by physical food alone. What Jesus is saying to me is, "If I allow this mind to be in me that was also in Christ Jesus, I am going to feed on the Word of God so that I am spiritually alert and awake at all times."

No one can go for a full month without physical food and not feel the effects of food deprivation. Most people can't miss one meal without craving food. We have been trained to eat daily. Our bodies are geared for regular food intake. Our bodies will rebel loudly if we don't give them nourishment.

Some Irishmen recently proved that you can starve to death living only on prayer. They were going to fast until they got their own way. They fasted; they died.

Little babies wouldn't last very long if we didn't accept the responsibility of feeding them. The same thing is true in our spiritual lives. God shows us in the physical life what happens to us in the spiritual life if we behave the same way in both areas.

We cannot get along with just an occasional dose of physical food. By the same token, we cannot get along with just an occasional dose of spiritual food.

Our spirits will starve. We need to eat the Word of God every day.

There are times when I have an opportunity to read more than I do at other times. There are other times when there are so many time-consuming situations that I don't get to read as much as I would like. I begin to feel spiritually starved if I am not in the Word of God. Give me three, four, or five hours in the Word of God, and suddenly I can feel myself coming alive again. The world becomes sunshiny. The earth turns warm and rosy, and I am sitting right on top of it.

The Word of God inside of you will cause you to grow and grow. You cannot survive as a Christian if you don't continue to feed and feed and feed on the Word of God. One day you will look back and realize that instead of being a crawling, colicky baby Christian, you have become a full grown adult spiritual giant.

Jesus believed the Word. I believe the Word. The more I eat, the more I grow and the more I can utilize the mind of Christ. If I spend more and more time with Him, He spends more and more time with me. If I relinquish my will more and more to Him, He can use me more and more to do His work.

Through salvation, we have been given one of the greatest gifts imaginable: the mind of Christ. Let us become so aware of His thinking in all areas and know what His thought patterns are that we will operate more fully as He desires us to act.

In the following chapters of this book, I have tried to paint a living picture of what our minds will be thinking on subjects that were dear to the heart of Jesus! For years this book has been a flame burning in my heart. I pray I can pass this flame on to you.

Unless one is born of water and the Spirit, he cannot enter the kingdom of God.
—John 3:5

Two

Born Again

———————●———————

The expression "born again" has been used very loosely over the last few years, and it is easy to see why many people do not actually understand what the term means. When we are born again, we acquire the mind of Christ, and when we truly believe that, only then will our thinking begin to line up with His.

This term has scriptural roots. We read in John,

After dark one night a Jewish religious leader named Nicodemus, a member of the sect of the Pharisees, came for an interview with Jesus. "Sir," he said, "we all know that God has sent you to teach us. Your miracles are proof enough of this." Jesus replied, "With all the earnestness I possess I tell you this: Unless you are born again, you can never get into the Kingdom of God." "Born again!" exclaimed Nicodemus. "What do you mean? How can an old man go back into his mother's womb and be born again?" Jesus replied, "What I am telling you so earnestly is this: Unless one is born of water and the Spirit, he cannot enter the Kingdom of God. Men can only reproduce human life, but the Holy Spirit gives new life from heaven; so don't be surprised at my statement that you must be born again!" (*John 3:1–7 TLB*)

According to the dictionary, to be born means to be brought into life or existence. When we are born physically, we are brought into life in the world where we now live. We are at the same time brought into an existence that will last for a certain number of years on this earth. When we are born physically, we undergo a complete change of environment, thinking, acting, and behavior. We go from a total dependence upon our mother's body to a growing dependence upon ourselves.

To be born again is in many ways the same thing as being born the first time. When we are born again, our behavior changes, our thinking changes, our actions change, and most of the time even our environment changes.

That doesn't mean we have to move out of the house in which we are living when we are born again, but our associations (environment) change because we no longer have a desire to go to the places where we formerly had fun. We no longer enjoy the people with whom we previously associated, because we possess a new way of thinking and a brand new set of values. We go from a total dependence of one form, upon our own brain power, to a total dependence of another form, upon the power of God. We are going to think like new creatures.

One Bible translation says that unless a man is actually or honestly born again, he cannot "see" the kingdom of God. This means that we cannot know the kingdom of God; we cannot even become acquainted with the kingdom of God until we are actually born again by the Spirit of God.

Many people say, "Just saying a prayer makes you born again." While there are many people who have been born again by praying a very simple prayer, unless a change has come into their lives and they are actually able to "see" the kingdom of God, or the kingdom of heaven, they are not truly born again.

I vividly remember one of the things I said the first time I ever gave my testimony. "The day I was saved, I believe God opened the windows of heaven and gave me a glimpse of what eternity was all about, and from that day on, I have never wanted anything of this earth."

This same experience applies to every born again believer. When you are truly born again, you "see" the kingdom of God. It is not an actual physical thing, but in the supernatural you see that God has called you to a life that is above and beyond the life you are now experiencing.

Once we have truly seen the kingdom of God, there will never be "backsliding" or going backwards. There should be no desire to return to the things of this world because we have caught a glimpse of that perfect hope, which is the eternal kingdom of God.

Looking again at the fifth verse, we see that Jesus said, *"Unless one is born of water and the Spirit, he cannot enter the Kingdom of God"* (TLB). Because we have let His mind be in us, we are going to believe exactly the same way. We are not going to let our carnal minds come into play and say, "Well, I have gone to church all of my life. I have joined my church. I have said the church creed." Those things have nothing to do with being born again.

Jesus said, "Unless a man is born again, he cannot see the kingdom of God." Because we have allowed this mind to be in us that was also in Christ Jesus, we are going to agree one hundred percent with Jesus that we must be born again by God's Spirit before we can actually see the kingdom of heaven. Yet once we have truly been born again by God's Spirit, we will be able to see into that spiritual realm with our recreated spirits, or that new man that has risen up within us. We are going to shed the old clothes, the old robes, and we are going to put on the new ones, because we are new creatures in Christ.

Second Corinthians 5:17 tells us, *"Therefore, if anyone is in Christ, he is a new creation; old things have passed away; behold, all things have become new."*

We are new creatures in Christ. We are sparkling new lights in the kingdom of God. We are transformed from the old persons we used to be into the recreated persons that we now are. We should have no desire to do the things we formerly did, because the old things have all passed away and all things have become new (v. 17).

We are going to *act* like new creatures!

We are going to *think* like new creatures!

We are going to *speak* like new creatures!

To go back into sin, the old way of life, would be the same principle as a grown man saying, "I want to go back into my mother's womb because it was so nice and warm, and I felt so secure there." Once you are born, you are no longer that little baby floating in the water sack in the womb. You are an individual who is now living in the world, and you can never go back.

The same thing is true of a genuine born-again experience. We have no right, nor should we have a desire, to go back to the old things of the sinful world and continue participating in the old ways of life. Before I was born again, I smoked, drank, cussed, and told dirty jokes. I certainly was not an example of someone possessing the mind of Christ; however, once I was born again, I became a new creation and the *"old things"* (v. 17) passed away!

Why Are Some Saved and Others Not?

Over and over I have pondered this one question. Why is it that some people become new creations, and some people don't? Why is it that some people never seem to have trouble in their Christian lives, and others never seem to get over the hurdles?

There are many things that tie together to make the Christian life simple and easy. It all goes back to the genuine born-again experience. Being born again is not an emotional experience where we cry and are drained emotionally, only to get up from an altar and live the same way we did previously.

We know that an individual cannot come to Jesus unless the Spirit of God draws him, but once the Spirit draws him, the responsibility for the effectiveness of the born-again experience rests upon the person himself.

Salvation is not a decision of the emotions; salvation is a decision of the will. Emotions are often the result of a genuine born-again experience, but are not always indicative of a genuine experience.

Genuine salvation comes from our own wills.

Until we can honestly say, "I will to follow after Jesus; I will to be obedient to God; I will to walk away from sin; I will to be the person that God wants me to be," our salvation can be wishy-washy and on-again, off-again.

When we truly make this decision of our wills, we have done our part; then Jesus does His part. The Spirit of Jesus merges with, or comes into, our spirits. We are conceived by the Holy Spirit; God plants His Seed, Jesus, and His life, into our spirits, and from that Seed, Jesus, we are born spiritually. Rom. 8:9 says, *"And remember that if anyone doesn't have the Spirit of Christ living in him, he is not a Christian at all"* (TLB).

The glorious day when Jesus became my Savior and Lord, I willed to follow Him. I looked up to God and said, "God, I'll make a deal with You. I'll give You all of me for all of You!"

God took me up on the deal that I offered Him, and even though I got the best of the deal, the decision of my own intellect and mind has kept me on the Christian road for all these years. I have lived without ever backsliding, without ever questioning or doubting God, without ever wondering if the Christian life really worked, and without ever wanting to return to the old life.

I made a decision that was not forced by emotions, a song, or a religious atmosphere. It was a decision that I had clearly thought about for months while I was attending a Bible-preaching church. It was a decision that had been made before I went to church on a particular Sunday morning. I looked at what the Devil had to offer and at what God had to offer. I liked God's offer much better! So, with my own free will, I deliberately chose to follow God.

Throughout His lifetime, Jesus always chose to follow God's will for His life. Even at the cross, He never questioned that God's will would override any human emotions He might have.

Heaven Cannot Be Earned

There is always a delicate balance between "works" and "grace," because works are insufficient to secure salvation. Please do not feel that I am trying to say that you can earn your way into heaven, because I tried that for years via the tuna-fish-and-cream-cheese-sandwich bit and washing dishes in the church basement after congregational dinners. It doesn't work. We know that

> *by grace you have been saved through faith, and that not of yourselves; it is the gift of God, not of works, lest anyone should boast. For we are His workmanship, created in Christ Jesus for good works, which God prepared beforehand that we should walk in them.* (Eph. 2:8–10)

Good works will follow the believer, but the works alone won't save the unbeliever.

The Critical Role of the Will

Every day we are confronted with opportunities to will to be obedient to God, or to will to be disobedient. Every action in which we are involved is an opportunity to do what God wants us to do or an occasion to make a decision not to obey Him. Where we go, what we listen to, what we read, what we watch, what we hear, and what we see are daily opportunities for us to be obedient to what God tells us in His Word. That is why when a person has a genuine born-again experience, it is easy for him to be obedient to God, because he possesses the mind of Christ and will want to do the same things Jesus did.

Jesus never even considered disobeying His Father. He had the mind of God. When we follow Jesus with all our hearts, we will have the mind of God.

If we have not willed to make a complete and total commitment of our lives (and it is definitely a decision of one's own will), we are going to have problems throughout our Christian lives. There is no way we can walk with one foot in the Spirit and the other foot in the Devil's territory.

A beautiful Scripture that puzzled me for years was recently made plain by the Holy Spirit, and it fits in so perfectly with what Jesus thinks about being born again.

Matthew 9:16–17 reads,

No one puts a piece of unshrunk cloth on an old garment; for the patch pulls away from the garment, and the tear is made worse. Nor do they put new wine into old wineskins, or else the wineskins break, the wine is spilled, and the wineskins are ruined. But they put new wine into new wineskins, and both are preserved.

The second verse pertains to becoming the new creatures in Christ when we are truly born again. It plainly shows the ridiculousness and futility of trying to live a Christian life while still living in sin. You cannot cram the new birth experience into a life that is still interested in the things of the flesh, because the penalty is that it will burst at the seams; the end result will be worse than your life was in the beginning.

When you put the new wine, new life—which is the new birth experience—into your life, it has to be put into a vessel that is clean and pure. You may say, "Well, when I asked God to forgive my sins, didn't He forgive them?" Yes, He did, but if you will to go your own way and you will to do your own thing, your temple is going to be cluttered up again immediately with sin. Then the new wine, or the new birth experience, and the old wineskins, or the old life, are both ruined, and you are worse off than before. However, when you will to be a new creature in Christ and you will to be a new creature in your physical being, then both are preserved.

It is impossible to be truly born again without a commitment of your will to God and a decision to stop following after the dictates of your flesh. The most miserable people in the world are those who have said a sinner's prayer and then have gone back to their old ways of living. The miserable, pathetic churchgoer who says, "I just can't give up cigarettes because I still like to smoke" is far more miserable than the individual who has never said a sinner's prayer, but just goes on enjoying being a sinner.

It is just as hard to be a halfway Christian as it is to try to make a new patch hold on an old pair of jeans. You put new material on top, but the threads underneath are so worn out that they won't hold the threads of the new one.

How to Enjoy Christianity

Colossians 3:23 tells us one of the easiest ways to enjoy Christianity to its fullest: *"And whatever you do, do it heartily, as to the Lord and not to men."*

"Do it heartily" means that we should never be halfhearted in anything we do for the Lord. Jesus tells us in Revelation what's going to happen to us if we are: *"I know your works, that you are neither cold nor hot. I could wish you were cold or hot.*

So then, because you are lukewarm, and neither cold nor hot, I will vomit you out of My mouth" (Rev. 3:15–16).

Because we have allowed this mind to be in us that was also in Christ Jesus, let's get red-hot, on fire for the Lord, because that was Jesus' lifestyle. Jesus said that unless we were born again, we could never get into the kingdom of God, so let's make sure that we are truly new creatures in Christ by making that decision with our wills to stop playing around and really get serious with God right now.

Let's say a prayer together to make sure you really are born again because you *will* to be a Christian!

> Father, I'm not interested in going to hell. I want to go to heaven. I ask You to forgive me and wash me in the precious blood of Jesus. Lord Jesus, with my mind, my intellect, and my will, I invite You to come into my heart and to make me the kind of person You want me to be. I will to follow You. I will to live above sin. I will to be obedient in everything You tell me to do. I will to serve You. I will to make a complete commitment of my life to You right now. Thank You for saving me and hearing my prayer. In Jesus' name.

Something happened to you in that split second of time when you were born again by the Spirit of God. When we fully realize what actually happens to us in that moment, it should be the most awe-inspiring thing that ever occurs in our lives.

Your Natural Mind Is God's Enemy

Many of us said a little sinner's prayer in the past, but since we did not have any teaching up to that point, we didn't understand what really happened to us. Because the world doesn't teach us the things of God, the carnal mind is at enmity with God (Rom. 8:7) and cannot understand the things of the Spirit.

In one split second, we jump from a sinner's world with a natural mind into the Spirit's world with all the supernatural activities of God. In other words, God still operates through us as human beings, but He does it in such a super way that it becomes a supernatural way.

There is a supernatural thing that takes place within us when we are born again. We no longer belong to the Devil. We belong to God. We no longer operate with the mind of a sinner because we have been given the mind of Christ. Now we have to learn to utilize the wisdom of Jesus and thus operate with His mind in control.

God doesn't say, "After you have been saved six months, I will allow you to *'let this mind be in you which was also in Christ Jesus'* (Phil. 2:5)."

No, when you are born again, you become a *"new creation"* (2 Cor. 5:17). At that very moment, even though you may not act like it or feel like it, you really are a new creature with the mind of Christ.

Some people have a very dramatic experience. They understand and know they are new persons with new chances at life. Others do not. It becomes a struggle until we learn that we just have to receive and act on what is given to us.

Let me give you a simple example of what I mean. I doubt if you remember when you were born in your natural life. Something very dramatic happened to you on that day when you actually became a separate person operating independently of your mother. Until that time, you were depending on the food and the strength and the nourishment in your mother's body to give you the necessary substances to grow.

Once you entered the world and that umbilical cord was cut, a drastic change took place. No longer could you depend on your mother in the same involuntary way as you had before. You had to look to outside sources for nourishment. No longer did you have all of your life-giving substance flowing into your body through the umbilical cord.

Suddenly, you became a little entity all by yourself. Probably all you did was cry, scream, holler, and sleep in between meals. Oh, you could wiggle your hands and feet, but your productive activity was very limited.

I like to compare an infant's development with the Christian life. The moment you are born again, that umbilical cord to the Devil is cut. You have been fed by the Devil up until the time you were born again. Once that cord is cut, he can no longer feed you his lies. You have become a separate and special person in the kingdom of God.

Many people think they should be spiritual giants and fully mature right off the bat. Rarely does that happen. I have never known a child who came out of his mother's womb walking and leaping and praising God. When you are born again, it is the same growing-up principle that applies to your physical development.

There are some things that are natural for us to do as babies. Crying is a natural reflex babies use to communicate with the world that they are uncomfortable—wet, cold, hot, or hungry. As soon as their needs are met, they go off to sleep.

But what happens if they have been given the wrong food? Have you ever heard of colic? Many babies have it at one time or another. But do you know what? They all grow out of it.

Compare this to the Christian life. We talk, listen, read, eat, and sleep as baby Christians. But what happens if we don't get enough to eat? Perhaps we eat something that we aren't able to digest. Perhaps we eat the wrong food and get sick. I call this "Christian colic."

Sometimes things get so complicated that we think, "Oh, I can't understand this. I don't understand this, so I can't possibly live the Christian life."

All you really have is a case of Christian colic, and you need to keep on a bit further. You'll get over that Christian colic. No child ever grew up into his adult years continuing to have colic. Rare is the child who ever has it after he reaches two years of age.

The same thing should be true in our Christian lives. As baby Christians, maybe we are entitled to a little Christian colic once in awhile when we are first born again by the Spirit of God. However, we need to get over it and go on in the Lord, growing and reaching out to others. We no longer should be lying there in our comfortable baby beds screaming, hollering, kicking, and fussing.

Just as babies practice walking, we must practice the spiritual laws God has given to us. Babies trip, fall down, and bruise their knees, as well as their noses, as they learn to walk. But they don't stay down. Young children see the exciting things adults are doing and are determined to act like "big people" do.

Baby Christians have to do the same thing. Get your eyes on Jesus and allow *"this mind* [to] *be in you which was also in*

Christ Jesus" (Phil. 2:5). You may fall down, make mistakes, bruise your ego, and have your nose bent, but you have been given all the tools necessary to grow and develop in the Christian life. Just as in human development, however, if you don't exercise your arms, legs, and voice, they will shrivel, die, and be useless.

Get busy and exercise your spiritual muscles!

God willed to make known what are the riches of the glory of this mystery among the Gentiles: which is Christ in you, the hope of glory.
—Colossians 1:27

Three

Christ in You, the Hope of Glory

●

The book of John is probably the greatest of all of the Gospels in line with what Paul preached: *"Christ in you, the hope of glory"* (Col. 1:27). Jesus said some tremendous things about Himself being the *"true vine"* and the Father the true *"vinedresser"* in John 15:1.

"Every branch in Me that does not bear fruit He takes away.... *Abide in Me, and I in you"* (vv. 2, 4). It's a two-way proposition. We abide in Him, and He abides in us! I looked up the word *abide,* and it means "to go into." To go into something means to be so wholly submerged that there is no part of you left over at all.

Jesus said, *"Abide in Me, and I in you. As the branch cannot bear fruit of itself, unless it abides in the vine, neither can you, unless you abide in Me"* (v. 4).

Jesus is saying to us that if we do not *"abide"* in Him, we cannot have the fruit and the fruitfulness He wants us

43

to have. He said, *"Unless you abide in Me"* (v. 4), or unless we "go into" Him so totally and so completely that our own self-natures wholly disappear, then we can have much fruit. Without Him, we can have nothing.

He proceeds to say, *"If anyone does not abide in Me, he is cast out as a branch and is withered; and they gather them and throw them into the fire, and they are burned"* (v. 6). But verse 7 in that chapter contains some powerful words: *"If you abide in Me* [go into Me], *and My words abide in you* [go into you], *you will ask what you desire, and it shall be done for you."*

What a promise of God! Anything and everything we want will be done, will be accomplished, will be given, if we just so much as desire it, if we will just so completely immerse ourselves in Him and "go into Him" that there will be absolutely no recognition of what we used to be before we became Christians.

Jesus also said,

> *As the Father loved Me, I also have loved you; abide in My love. If you keep My commandments, you will abide in My love, just as I have kept My Father's commandments and abide in His love.*   *(John 15:9–10)*

He wants us to "go into" His love, so that we will experience in our own lives a love that is above and beyond anything we would ever be capable of doing in the natural. He wants us to do so in order that His joy may remain in us. He wants us to have His joy operating at top speed within us at all times.

Once when T. L. and Daisy Osborn were at our home, we were all talking about *"Christ in you, the hope of glory"* (Col. 1:27). I mentioned to T. L. that the first thing I ever learned as a brand-new baby Christian was that Jesus Christ lived in me. He was surprised that it was clear to me so quickly because when he was a young minister and preached that Jesus lived in him, many thought he was a heretic.

Everyone should understand that Jesus actually does live in us.

If we can get to the point where we totally, completely, and positively believe that Jesus is living inside us, walking through our feet, working through our hands, and speaking through our lips, it will do a lot to eliminate the problems that sometimes develop in our Christian lives. Honestly, those problems come because we don't understand the simple principle of *"Christ in you, the hope of glory,"* and our need of abiding in Him with all of His glory, His power, and His majesty.

His Ability within Us

It is such an incredible and absolutely overwhelming thought to realize that we actually have the ability of God within us because Jesus said, *"All authority—all power of rule—in heaven and on earth has been given to Me"* (Matt. 28:18 AMP), and then Jesus turned right around and said to us, *"Behold! I have given you authority and power to trample upon serpents and scorpions, and (physical and mental strength and ability) over all the power that the enemy (possesses), and nothing shall in any way harm you"* (Luke 10:19 AMP).

Sometimes it is difficult to describe the actual experience of knowing that you know that you know that Jesus Christ is living big inside of you. It can be tough explaining how you walk in faith and believe that Jesus is actually living within, yet this knowledge gives you unlimited power!

We should never preach the Gospel if we cannot do the Gospel. If we really believe Jesus lives inside of us, then we ought to be able to do everything that was done in the Bible.

Christians live far below the level of where God wants them to live. We seek the lesser things, we are satisfied with the lesser things, and we fail to reach up and to reach out into those higher heights of glory into the world of the unknown, into the world of the unseen, into the world that has never really been tampered with!

God wants us to reach out to a new world! He wants us all to operate in the supernatural. When we really believe Jesus Christ is living in and through us in the power of the Holy Spirit, we will be loaded with *enteos,* which means enthusiasm. It means God within. When you have Jesus Christ living in you, you are going to be enthusiastic! God within equals enthusiasm. I have never known anyone who could prove to me that he was really a Christian if he wasn't excited about Jesus and what Jesus has done in his life. I have never seen a deadpan Christian. I have seen a lot of deadpan people, but never a deadpan Christian.

Salvation Releases Enthusiasm

What are we going to be enthusiastic about? If Jesus lives within, we're going to be enthusiastic about our salvation. The very first thing you are going to be enthusiastic about is the fact that Jesus Christ is living in you. If you are truly saved, you will be excited about what Jesus has done in your life. The reason I am so wild and excited all of the time is that I allowed Jesus to do things in my life. Did you notice that I said, "I *allowed* Him"? God never forces you to do a thing.

46

I fell so madly in love with Jesus that down the drain went the cigarettes, the alcohol, and all of those horrible habits that I had before I got saved. I am excited about salvation because salvation gave me the power to be the kind of person God wants me to be instead of the kind of woman the Devil wants me to be. Many people hang onto the Devil even after they think they are saved because they are not willing to let God make those changes in their lives that need to be made. I guarantee you that any change God wants to make within us is for the better. Everything He does is an improvement in our lives!

Many people say, "Oh, I have to give up this." No, you don't have to give up a thing. He lifts you above the desire to do the things you did before you got saved! That is why I am so excited about salvation. It gave me a new outlook.

I became a *"new creation"* (2 Cor. 5:17). I became a new creature. My mind was renewed. No longer did I have the old dirty, filthy mind that I had before I got saved. That is why I am so excited about salvation, because Jesus Christ living within me makes me bubble up and just burst with excitement over what He has done for me!

We are also going to be excited about healing the sick. We are not only going to be excited; we are going to be superexcited!

Before I received the baptism with the Holy Spirit, something happened that I will never forget. A man walked up to me in St. Petersburg, Florida, and said, "God has given you the gift of healing. Why don't you use it?" Before I had a chance to open my mouth, he just plain disappeared right in front of my eyes (I wonder if he was an angel). Whoever it was, I have never forgotten that very special moment when someone said, "You have the gift of healing." That stayed in my mind, and I thought, "Wow! Could that ever happen to me?"

Especially during the holiday season, I look at some of the unhappy faces of people in the grocery store, in the shopping center, and in the mall. These people are frantically racing around, trying to find the answer to life. Running, running, running, running, looking, looking, looking! Why? Because they have not yet found the answer to life. They haven't found that *"Christ in you"* (Col. 1:27) is the only true source of glory! We don't have to be running, running, running, constantly trying to find the answer. We have it! That's why we can be enthusiastic, because God within us makes it possible.

When I got saved, Jesus opened my mouth, and I haven't shut it since! And I don't intend to shut it, because it is that *enteos* within me that makes it impossible to talk about anything else except Jesus.

Jesus in us will allow us to become the new creatures that we are promised. We are not going to be digging up the garbage of the past, saying, "Oh, but I had all these awful things in the past." Who cares? Quit bragging about your past. Start talking about who you are now and what Jesus did for you.

We are going to believe in our new life, and we are going to believe in our new creation.

Concentration Releases Growth

We are not going to concentrate on problems. We are not going to talk about them, because talking about problems makes them grow and grow and grow and grow! Pretty soon we are overwhelmed by problems. Get your mind off the problems and on the answer. When you begin thinking about

Jesus and what God has done in your life, your problems are just going to slip away, disappear, and be as though they never were.

The Jesus in us has a hunger for the Word of God. The more we get into God's Word, the more we discover that as we begin to grow, we begin to rise and rise and rise. Our problems don't rise with us. The problems stay way down there. But as we rise, we get further and further away from our problems, until suddenly they are so insignificant that we can't see them anymore.

One of the best examples I know of in this area happens when you ride in a plane. When you first take off from the airport, you look out the window and you can see everything plainly and in clear detail, but the higher the plane rises, the smaller the houses become.

The same thing is true with your spiritual life. As you begin to go into those spiritual realms, the problems get smaller, smaller, and smaller, until suddenly they are so little you cannot see them anymore.

"Christ in you, the hope of glory" is going to make you excited about the power of God to overcome in every area in your life!

The time is fulfilled, and the kingdom of God is at hand.
Repent, and believe in the gospel.
—Mark 1:15

Four

Repentance

———•———

Charles and I are blessed to have an exciting ministry that goes around the world. It is an international ministry that touches the lives of people not only in the United States, but also in many other nations. As a result, we receive mail from people of diverse cultural, social, economic, and ethnic backgrounds.

Surprisingly, the contents of these letters say the same thing. A letter sent from a city here in the United States will be similar to a letter sent from a city in Europe.

After a while we began to notice a pattern in the needs expressed by people in their letters and discovered that specific spiritual problems are not confined to any particular locale. One problem in particular is mentioned repeatedly all over the world. It seems that people everywhere are struggling and failing in their attempts to live a Christian life. But, as far as we can determine from their mail, these people are tripping over "step one" of living an overcoming, victorious, fulfilled life as a believer.

That step is repentance.

Recently, I read a letter from a lady in Queensland, Australia, that was amazingly similar to a letter I had just read from someone in Nigeria. Another letter from a man in Indianapolis, Indiana, was almost the same. They were all saying, "I want to love God, and I want to walk the Christian way. I am trying to lead a good moral life, but what is the matter with me?" In each case the writers of the letters desperately wanted to serve God, but their lives seemed empty and cold, and they could not see the manifestation of God in their personal situations. Each one literally broke my heart.

Each letter also had another similarity. All of the writers wrote that they had said the sinner's prayer many times (one even wrote that she had prayed it about fifty times), but they had not seen any results from their prayers. Their lives seemed to just go on as before with no real life, no hungering for the Word of God or the things of God, and they were as defeated as they had been before the prayers.

In Matthew 4:17 we read, *"From that time Jesus began to preach and to say, 'Repent, for the kingdom of heaven is at hand'"* (emphasis added). That is the important step the people from Australia, Nigeria, Indiana, and all over the world have missed in entering into the type of Christian life the Word of God exemplifies.

Mark 1:14–15 says the same thing. It states, *"Now after John was put in prison, Jesus came to Galilee, preaching the gospel of the kingdom of God, and saying, 'The time is fulfilled, and the kingdom of God is at hand. Repent, and believe in the gospel'"* (emphasis added). Once again the Word of God instructs us in the process of spiritual growth. Not only did Jesus say to repent, but also to believe.

The dictionary defines *repentance* as, "to feel pain, sorrow, or regret for something that one has done, or left undone; to be conscience stricken or contrite; to change one's mind about some past action, intention in consequence, or regret or dissatisfaction." It goes on to say that the theological meaning of the word is, "to feel sorrow for sin as leads to amendment of one's ways, to be penitent."

Let me show you what the Word of God says about repentance. Researching the word *repentance* in Hebrew and Greek, I found there are eight words describing repentance. These eight words, four in Hebrew and four in Greek, give us the total picture of true Bible repentance. There are different places in Scripture where each of these meanings is used for a specific purpose.

The first *repent* in Hebrew is *nacham,* which means "to sigh or to breathe strongly or to be sorry." In this type of repentance, one is sorry for something he has done. For example, if you put your life's savings in a particular stock that had shown tremendous gain, only to suddenly see it go right down to the bottom and be worthless, you would be very sorry. You would regret having put all of your money into what turned out to be a bad investment. This is a form of repentance, by avoiding something because you have discovered by experience that it wasn't a wise thing to do.

Another Hebrew word for repentance is *shuwb,* which means "to turn back." It means not repeating something because you have learned that there is a consequence to it, such as touching a hot stove. Any young child can testify to that kind of repentance. Once he has been burned, he will be careful to avoid contact with the flame so that it won't happen again.

The third Hebrew word for repentance, *nocham,* is particularly interesting. It means "to regret" rather than repent.

The sorrow is connected with being found out rather than for committing the sin.

An excellent example of *nocham* is a person who robs a bank. If he successfully accomplished the robbery, made a fast getaway, leaving no fingerprints or identification behind, and lived his life in prosperity to the end of his days, there would be no repentance.

But if the person was caught and sent to prison, he would "regret" his action. This is proven by the fact that many prisoners repeat their crimes as soon as they are released, which indicates no repentance or turning away, but a desire to do it again and not get caught!

Compassion is the meaning of the fourth Hebrew word for repentance. It is *nichum* and is an emotional concern for other people. When we acquire the nature of God, because we have been created in the very image of God, we should acquire the compassion of Jesus. But just because you feel sorry for someone else does not mean you truly repent for what you have done in your life. There are a lot of organizations that are not Christian, but operate out of compassion for other people. Many collect food and clothing and give away Christmas baskets and toys because of their compassion. That type of compassion is admirable, but it is not repentance.

In the Greek language the word *metanoa* means "to change your mind for the better or to change your attitude toward sin." This is strictly a mental change of mind. It is "sense" knowledge that says, "I am going to straighten up my life. It is not good for me to be smoking cigarettes, because the Surgeon General's report said it could be harmful, so I am going to quit smoking." It means to change your own mind.

Someone who is poor might say, "I have lived in poverty long enough. I don't like poverty, so I am going to be something different from now on. I am going to make some money for myself."

A Changed Mind Equals a Changed Life

I said those words myself many, many years ago before I ever got saved. I was raised in abject poverty, and somewhere along the line, I decided I was going to be rich. It didn't matter how long or how hard I had to work, I was going to get some money. From the time I was seventeen years old, I worked at least two jobs at a time, sometimes 12, 14, 16, or even 18 hours a day, for one reason: I wanted money. I had changed my mind about being poor and was willing to work and do everything required to rise above my poverty. But that kind of repentance has nothing to do with true repentance, which totally changes your life.

The sixth Greek word for repentance is *metamelomai,* which means "to regret the consequence of sin, not the cause of sin." This type of repentance was clearly illustrated to Charles and me not too long ago.

We received a frantic telephone call from a young man we had known for several years. The young man was in jail. "Please, come and get me out," he pleaded.

"What did you do to get arrested?" I asked.

"Nothing," he replied. "My car broke down on the highway, and I was trying to repair it when the police came by and began to accuse me of doing something illegal. Now they have put me in jail and won't even let me post bond."

We were very concerned about the young man, but his explanation about his arrest didn't make much sense. Policemen don't indiscriminately arrest people without a reason. Although we wanted to help the young man, we did not have the freedom from the Holy Spirit to rush down to jail and try to get him out.

God gives you connections when you need connections and keeps you from going off the deep end to help someone who perhaps should not be helped at that particular time. Through a friend in the police department, we discovered that the young man was not innocently hauled into jail as he had claimed, but was charged with being caught in a homosexual act. The young man had lied to us just to use our influence to get himself out of jail. He was not sorry at all for what he had done, but was sorry he had been caught. He wanted a quick, easy way out of the situation.

Repentance: Key to Deliverance

This response seems to be common, we have noticed, in homosexual behavior. It is sometimes difficult for homosexuals to totally turn around and be changed into the image of God, because they only regret the consequences of their sin. They regret the fact that they are found out, but deep down in their hearts, they do not regret the act itself. That is because they have never really genuinely repented of the sin of homosexuality in their lives.

This type of repentance—being sorry only for the consequence of sin—also applies to other areas. For example, speeding. Have you ever received a ticket for going over the speed limit? Did it make you more conscious of the law and help you stay within the allowable speed?

I was stopped once for rushing through a stop sign. When the policeman pulled up alongside the car, I realized instantly why I was being stopped. "I didn't come to a dead stop at that stop sign, did I?" I confessed as he walked over to my car. He laughed heartily at my total honesty. In fact, he didn't even write me a ticket because I was sincerely sorry for what I had done. Even to this day when I come to a stop sign, I totally stop, pray in tongues, and proceed cautiously. My repentance for failure to abide by the law that says come to a complete stop at a stop sign caused me to change my ways.

There are some people I know (I'm sure you can recall some, too) who have had one speeding ticket right after the other. That says, "I am only sorry I got caught. I am only sorry I had to pay big, big fines because I was going 85 miles an hour in a 55-miles-per-hour speed zone." That is not repentance. Instead, that person becomes more careful in watching his rearview mirror than watching his speed. No Christian should ever get a speeding ticket. And if he does, it should make him repentant enough to change his driving habits to comply with local, state, and federal laws.

God's Word tells us to obey the law. I don't have to worry about checking the rearview mirror; all I have to be concerned with is God, and He knows whether I am going over the speed limit or not. Some people think I don't drive fast enough, that I am slow. It takes me a little longer to get there, but I get there. God has angels around my car. Hallelujah! The angels get off when you drive over the speed limit, so I would rather drive the speed limit and make sure they stay there!

What keeps most people walking the "straight and narrow"? Sometimes they walk that way not just because they want to, but because they are afraid of the consequences if they don't. Many people would go out and rob a bank if they thought they could get away with it. Many would steal from stores if they knew no one would find out. Occasionally, it is reported in the newspapers that someone has embezzled money from a company or bank, or misappropriated funds in some other way. When they are found out, the people who have committed these deeds are sorry not for the deed itself, but for the fact they were discovered.

Desire Righteous Fruit

As Christians we should always be meticulously honest in all business dealings, not because we have to, but because we want to. The Holy Spirit within us will act as an umpire to make sure that when we have acted discreditably, we can ask for forgiveness, correct our action, and get back on course.

In the two Scriptures I referred to earlier, the word for repentance that Jesus used was the word *metanoia,* which signifies a real change of mind, an attitude toward sin, not merely the consequences of it. In other words, one might sincerely say, "Oh, God, I am sorry I said this or did that."

This matter of true repentance—or lack of true repentance—is evidenced in the many letters Charles and I receive. People say that their lives are defeated, but they don't really know why. They think the promises of God don't work in their lives. They ask, but they don't receive. They give, but they don't prosper. "Why?" they wonder. God has clearly shown me that the reason people are defeated, and the promises of God seemingly don't work in their lives, is that they do not truly repent.

God's promises, whether abundant life, blessings, or prosperity, are all conditional on our obedience to His commands.

Many people say the sinner's prayer, but they stop right there. The Word of God says, *"Godly sorrow produces repentance leading to salvation"* *(2 Cor. 7:10).* I believe there are many defeated Christians because they never really understood what Jesus meant when He said, *"Repent."* He meant to turn your back on what you were doing.

This isn't merely giving something up to be a Christian. I never gave up one single thing! He lifted me above the desire to do these things. I was the wildest smoker, drinker, "cusser," and dirty joke teller you ever saw, until I met Jesus as Lord and Savior.

Being a Christian doesn't mean you have to give things up; it means you get to! You get to give up all those destructive habits and lifestyles that will hurt your life. And you get to give up that old, dead spirit man who is condemned to eternal damnation.

Many of you might look at me and find it hard to believe that before 1965 I was a wild sinner. My vocabulary would have shocked you. But a peculiar thing happened in my life. I did not say the sinner's prayer when I first heard the third chapter of John. I heard it and realized that I was not really born again. I thought I was a Christian. I went to church on Sundays. Even though I lived like the Devil the rest of the week, smoking, drinking and cursing, I thought going to church made me a Christian. What a shock it was to find out I had not really been born again!

But even though I realized I was not really saved, I was reluctant to make a decision. I continued to smoke, drink, and live my own life as I always had. But the Spirit of God continued to convict me and show me I was a sinner. About nine months later I cried out, "Oh, God, have mercy on me, a sinner!"

That day, God reached down and saved me. Not only had I called on God for mercy, but beneath the voice that asked for help was a heart that was broken and contrite. When God saved me, I knew I was saved. In fact, I was so euphoric that for about two days I didn't even know who I was! But I knew Jesus Christ was living in my heart! I remember thinking, "He's in there! He's in there!" Jesus was in my heart, so I slammed the door, locked it, threw away the key, and said, "Jesus, You can never get out of there!"

The very second I said that, my life began to change, not mildly, but drastically! I acquired a hungering for the Word of God and was sure that all Bibles would be confiscated before I finished reading the Book that had lain on a table in my house for such a long time, untouched by human hands! I wanted to find out everything God had to say! I could never get enough of God!

There was something special about nighttime. Maybe it was because I was away from the hustle and bustle of my printing company, away from the telephones, away from people, away from anything that would destroy the intimate relationship I was developing with God.

It seemed I would be engulfed in His love when I snuggled down into bed and turned the lights off. It was "Just you and me, Lord!" I would savor every precious minute of the love-relationship we were developing. My heart and soul cried out to please Him.

Night after night a pattern seemed to be developing. I began to remember all the things I had done from "little bitty" on. I remembered the penny I stole from my mother. I said, "Oh, God, I am sorry for that."

I was genuinely sorry. I wasn't sorry that I got caught. I was sorry I had sinned against God. While I do not think it is necessary for everyone to do this, I went back over my entire life; over and over again the same thing would happen. I would begin to sob. I would cry and cry and cry. Sometimes I would cry for two or three hours and couldn't even remember what I was crying about.

It was not a sad cry of remembering things like, "I lost my mother. I lost my father. I lost my husband before I was 35 years old." It was not that kind of a cry I cried on each of those occasions. It was a cry that was actually a "glad" cry. Somehow or other, I seemed to be sobbing from the innermost depths of my heart. I couldn't figure out what I was crying about, and yet, when I finished and finally fell asleep, I felt good. My body felt good, my soul felt good, and I just felt good all over. The next morning I would think, "I can't stay awake every night crying, so tonight I'll go right to sleep."

But when night came and I went to bed and began to love God and talk to Him in the quietness of the darkness, because that is always such a beautiful time to talk with God, I discovered I was doing the same thing over and over again.

I would say, "Oh, God, I love You. Thank You for saving me. Thank You for forgiving me of all my sins. Oh, God, I am truly and sincerely sorry for everything wrong I have ever done." Then I would begin to think of a lot more things, and I would start all over again. I am sure I told God about things that He didn't even think were a sin anyway, but I believe I thought of everything I had ever done in my entire life.

I thought of the most peculiar things you could ever imagine. But in my heart, I was genuinely sorry for anything and everything I had ever done from the day I was born until the day I got saved. It's amazing what the Holy Spirit brings back to your mind when you are truly repentant. I didn't know then what was happening to me in those nightly engagements I had with God, but today I know it was Holy Spirit tears that were cleansing me with godly sorrow for everything I had ever done against God!

I do not believe it is necessary for everybody to smell the garbage in his life before he is saved. In my case, I can see it was necessary that I bring it out to myself, because my biggest problem was that I had difficulty telling God I was a sinner. When He finally did show me and convince me that I was a sinner, I began to see all the things I had done in my life that I had refused to admit were sin.

When you are open to God, the Holy Spirit will bring to your remembrance many things. Each night I would remember something else, as if I was putting a searchlight into my innermost being. Once again, my body would be torn with sobs. It was a cry from the very depths of my heart as I sobbed and sobbed, telling God how sorry I was and promising Him I would never do it again.

That same type of repentance may not have happened to you, but I believe that churches need to preach more about repentance, because getting saved doesn't mean just saying a sinner's prayer. You will discover that you will walk the Christian road as God wants you to walk if there is true repentance in your heart. The condemnation most people have in their Christian lives is because they have not truly repented and turned the opposite direction.

Forget Your Past

The next most important thing is to go on and forget your past. We need to realize that our sins have not only been forgiven by God, but forgotten as well, because He buries them in the deepest sea, never to be remembered again. We need to accept the forgiveness of God in our lives, and go on from there.

God is not going to throw you out for some little sin you committed after you got saved. The minute you do something wrong, ask His forgiveness right then and there and never do it again. We don't need to worry unless we keep on doing the same thing over and over again. First John 1:9 says, *"If we confess our sins, He is faithful and just to forgive us and to cleanse us of all unrighteousness."*

The *Amplified Bible* states that verse this way:

> *If we [freely] admit that we have sinned and confess our sins, He is faithful and just [true to His own nature and promises] and will forgive our sins (dismiss our lawlessness) and continuously cleanse us from all unrighteousness—everything not in conformity to His will in purpose, thought and action.*

One of the things that amazes me about God is that if you said a sinner's prayer right now, and then five minutes later remembered some atrocious sin you had committed and said, "Oh, God, did you forgive me for that awful sin I committed 37 years ago?" God would say, "What sin?" because He doesn't even remember.

After I was saved, I cried for two or three months every night. All the nasty things I had ever said to anyone came back to my mind. I remember that I lied to a teacher when I was in the fourth grade. I thought to myself, "Oh, God, that was such a little lie." Then I realized there is no such thing as a little lie. All lies are big lies. I said, "Oh, God, I am sorry for that. I am sorry because I was the leader in the class, and I told a lie to the teacher." Then there would come those buckets of tears, the sobbing that racked my body, and then finally the peace of God!

What does repentance really mean? It means turning away, turning as fast as you can in the other direction, and going as fast as you can go away from sin.

Many people do not want to give up sin because they are not really sorry they sinned. Girls come to me over and over again when we are on the road and say something like this: "I want to say a sinner's prayer again. I want to ask God to forgive me. I went to bed with a boy last night and I knew I shouldn't have done it."

I say, "Did you ever do it before?"

Their answer is stereotyped: "Oh, yes, every Saturday night, every Wednesday night, too, and then Tuesday and Thursday with another guy, but I want to say a sinner's prayer again."

I guarantee you that kind of a person will be back at the altar the next Sunday because she will do the same thing all over again. Why? Because that individual was not genuinely sorry. The minute your heart really and truly repents, and you say, "Oh, God, I am sorry. I turn my back on that, and I will never do it again," that is the day when godly sorrow will come into your heart. And godly sorrow is the most joyful experience in the world because it leads to your eventual happiness in the Lord. I believe the reason I am so happy and free today is because of the repentance that came into my life—a repentance that said, "God, I will never, never do it again."

When I smoked my last cigarette, there was never a question of whether or not I was going to smoke again. I was sorry I had degraded the temple of God. Your body is definitely the holy temple of God, according to His Word (1 Cor. 6:19). I was so sorry because I could see those black lungs in my body full of "goop," and I was sorry I had ever done such a thing to God's temple. I believe that is the reason I have never been tempted by a cigarette from the day I was set free.

The same thing is true of alcohol. The day God set me free from alcohol, I was sorry I had ever had a drink in my life. I was sorry for the times I had become drunk. I was sorry! I repented with everything that was in me, and as a result of genuine repentance, I don't have enough strength in my hand today to lift one ounce of gin, whiskey, vodka, wine, or beer, because when you repent unconditionally and completely, there will never be a desire to do anything against God.

A Final Decision

The last Greek word is *ametameletos,* which means "irrevocable." In other words, "God, I am turning back. I am turning back. I will never walk that way again, because I have made an irrevocable decision, a decision that cannot be reversed or annulled." You may be *ametameletos* and not cry a tear; all you need is true repentance in your heart—godly sorrow.

Hebrews 4:12 states, *"For the word of God is living and powerful, and sharper than any two-edged sword, piercing even to the division of soul and spirit, and of joints and marrow, and is a discerner of the thoughts and intents of the heart."* We may fool ourselves sometimes in our motives or intentions, but God knows our hearts. He knows true repentance, and true repentance will launch you into the overcoming life you have desired.

I am going to ask you to do something special for yourself. When you go to bed tonight, say this prayer and mean it from the innermost parts of your being:

65

Father, I am not just saying a prayer. I am not just saying words. I am saying something from my heart. Lord, I am sorry for every avenue in my life that is not pleasing to You. I am sorry for those things of the world onto which I am still clinging. From this day forward, because I am repenting in my heart, I will turn around and go in the other direction. I will look to You for strength. I will look to You for power. I will never again look to myself. Forgive me for the things to which I have clung, and Lord Jesus, come into my clean and repentant heart to stay forever. Jesus, please possess me so that I can possess Your clean and pure mind!

"Create in me a clean heart, O God, and renew a steadfast spirit within me" (Ps. 51:10).

If you have faith as a mustard seed, you will say to this mountain, "Move from here to there," and it will move; and nothing will be impossible for you.
—Matthew 17:20

Five

Faith

———————●———————

Because we let the mind of Christ be in us, we should look upon faith exactly as Jesus does. Much has been said in recent years in an attempt to categorize and legalistically define faith. I know we have all heard sermons and sermons upon sermons describing faith, and I know we ourselves have given many talks on the subject of faith. However, let's take the word apart and look at it through the eyes of Jesus and with the mind of Christ.

If I were to make one simple, uncomplicated sentence describing faith, I would say that *faith is simply receiving what God says.* Meditate on that definition. Let your mind expand and go into all different directions to see if that doesn't really cover all that faith is. Faith is just having enough trust in God to believe in your heart everything He says, written or spoken. If you believe what God says, then you will be able to receive what He has for you.

Faith is not something that can be conjured up, nor can it be emotionalized to a point where it becomes more effective.

Emotionalism will oftentimes cause us to cross over into the area of presumption rather than allowing our own faith to develop and become strong.

The times in our lives when our faith has been the very strongest have not been super-hyperventilating times when we were sitting with a group of other believers begging and pleading with God for more faith. No, the greatest moments of our faith have been in the quiet solitude and constant knowledge of unquestioning belief that God is going to do what He says He will do.

Real faith is never something that is worked up. If you are honestly operating in faith, it will be a constantly solid, abiding calmness. It will produce joy and peace that permeates your very being to such a degree that there is no room at all left in your mind for any doubt or unbelief.

Doubt and unbelief are both opposites of faith. When we allow questions to come in, such as "Is this really God's will?" "Is God going to do it?" and "Am I really going to come out of this situation?" we are allowing doubts to come in that cause us to operate on the negative side of faith.

Jesus spoke very well about this in the eighth chapter of Matthew, starting with verse 5, which reads,

> *Now when Jesus had entered Capernaum, a centurion came to Him, pleading with Him, saying, "Lord, my servant is lying at home paralyzed, dreadfully tormented." And Jesus said to him, "I will come and heal him." The centurion answered and said, "Lord, I am not worthy that You should come under my roof. But only speak a word, and my servant will be healed. For I also am a man under authority, having soldiers under me. And I say to this one, 'Go,' and he goes; and to another,*

'Come,' and he comes; and to my servant, 'Do this,' and he does it." When Jesus heard it, He marveled, and said to those who followed, "Assuredly, I say to you, I have not found such great faith, not even in Israel! And I say to you that many will come from east and west, and sit down with Abraham, Isaac, and Jacob in the kingdom of heaven. But the sons of the kingdom will be cast out into outer darkness. There will be weeping and gnashing of teeth." Then Jesus said to the centurion, "Go your way; and as you have believed, so let it be done for you." And his servant was healed at that same hour. (Matt. 8:5–13)

Did you notice that Jesus said, *"I have not found such great faith, not even in Israel!"* Jesus was really commenting on this man's faith simply because he did not have to put on a show. He did not demand and command and say, "Now Jesus, You drop whatever You are doing, come down, and touch my servant." He had so much faith in the ability of God to perform through His Son Jesus Christ that he very calmly said, "You don't even have to go. You just speak the word, and it will be accomplished."

Seek God, and Faith Will Come Easily

The outstanding quality exhibited by the centurion is the fact that he had an unwavering, unmixed, undiluted, pure kind of faith. There was no doubt, no unbelief, no questioning, no nothing—except simple faith.

Jesus said to him, *"As you have believed."* That word *"believed"* covers a multitude of answers and non-answers to prayer because many people have tried to generate faith and have tried to confess faith instead of just believing and receiving what God has for them.

70

Since we possess the mind of Christ, how do we get our minds into a position where they will be capable of receiving the thoughts of God?

Jesus never questioned the *plan* of His Father.

Jesus never questioned the *ability* of His Father.

Jesus never questioned the *desire* of His Father.

He just believed His Father and was determined to do all that His Father sent Him to earth to accomplish. It wasn't simply the fact that the centurion made the statement, but he believed what he said. Many times we think we are stepping out in faith, but we don't really believe; we are just hoping that something good is going to happen.

Mark 4:37–41 tells about the great storm that arose when the disciples were in the boat with Jesus. The very first thing they said when the storm came up was, *"Teacher, do You not care that we are perishing?"* (v. 38). Jesus came right back at them and said, *"Why are you so fearful? How is it that you have no faith?"* (v. 40).

Jesus told His disciples very plainly that they didn't have any faith, because they were fearful when the problems came up. The same thing is true of us today. If we actually believe that we possess the mind of Christ, we are not going to be fearful in times of storms, distress, or troubles.

Notice that the man with the sick servant had no feelings of panic; he did not say, "You have to come right now. If You don't, my servant will die." He was very calm and said, *"Speak a word, and my servant will be healed"* (Matt. 8:8). However, fear, which is the opposite of faith, immediately came into the disciples. These two circumstances are wonderful examples of what happens when you believe and when you don't.

71

Let me ask you a question. If you were in a boat with Jesus and a big storm came up, would you be the least bit frightened? Not me, because I know I would be right there with the One who has *"all power...in heaven and in earth"* (Matt. 28:18 KJV).

Jesus had a lot to say about unbelief to His disciples. Matthew 17:14–21 is a good example of this. A man came to Jesus with an epileptic son and told Jesus that he had brought him to the disciples, but they could not cure him. Jesus rebuked the demon, and it came out of him. The child was cured. Then the disciples said, *"Why could we not cast it out?"* (v. 19). Jesus' answer to them was, *"Because of your unbelief"* (v. 20).

Unbelief and faith are two absolute opposites, and Jesus never had any unbelief in His mind, His heart, or His Spirit. But then look at what Jesus said. He didn't say, "If you had great big faith, you could have done it." He simply said, *"If you have faith as a mustard seed, you will say to this mountain, 'Move from here to there,' and it will move; and nothing will be impossible for you"* (v. 20).

Jesus is not saying to us that because we possess His mind we are going to possess great faith. He simply says, "Have that little tiny kind of faith that has no room for doubt and unbelief."

We need to begin to believe that it is not trying to manufacture, to weave, or to dream up an imaginary kind of faith, but it is simply getting back to little basic principles where we believe everything Jesus said.

To me, one of the most exciting examples in the entire Bible where faith is concerned (and I know there are many and each of us has a favorite) is the story of Shadrach, Meshach, and Abed-Nego.

Think of their simple faith when they replied to Nebuchadnezzar's question, *"But if you do not worship, you shall be cast immediately into the midst of a burning fiery furnace. And who is the god who will deliver you from my hands?"* (Dan. 3:15).

I love their answer. They said,

O Nebuchadnezzar, we have no need to answer you in this matter. If that is the case, our God whom we serve is able to deliver us from the burning fiery furnace, and He will deliver us from your hand, O king. (Dan. 3:16–17)

Look at what they said next: *"But if not, let it be known to you, O king, that we do not serve your gods, nor will we worship the gold image which you have set up"* (v. 18).

The thing that is so beautiful to me in this particular story is the fact that they were willing to give their lives to prove that God is God. Sometimes, to prove that, we have "hyperfaith"; we get out into an area where we think we are putting God on a spot so He will have to do what we want. In reality we are merely demonstrating a lack of faith.

I remember years ago there was a problem in the state of Mississippi where terrifying riots were going on between the blacks and the whites. A man walked out in front of a bulldozer and said, "God will protect me." But I have news for you. The bulldozer ran right over him and mashed him "flatter than a fritter" and killed him. He was obviously not operating under the blessing of God when he did this. However, Shadrach, Meshach and Abed-Nego had a relationship with God that was so firm that they experienced a supernatural miracle. They knew beyond a shadow of a doubt that they were coming out unharmed.

Faith or Fib?

Maybe your faith is like mine. There are times when I have faith for whatever situation is in front of me, and then there are times when my faith is not quite that strong. If I began to speak it and say I believed it, I would really, in effect, be telling a fib. But if I walk quietly, in my heart believing and trusting God for other things, little by little I have discovered that my faith will grow to the point where I will believe God for the thing I might not have been able to believe Him for one year, two years, three years, or ten years before.

One year when Charles and I were at PTL Club for their annual parade, two separate times God gave me simple faith to know that I had heard His voice, and both instances resulted in our seeing the glory of God.

On Sunday night there had been hundreds of tents all over that great Heritage USA complex, and it began thundering and lightning; the rain came down in buckets. It was like a monsoon. Can you imagine camping out in a tent with rivers of water two feet deep running through your tent?

By the next morning the tents had really disappeared. We had to get up at 5:15 A.M. to be at breakfast by 6:00 so that we could get information on the floats. We went downstairs, and it was still pouring down rain. It was some of the soggiest weather we had ever seen and was black as night outside.

The staff at PTL put us in vans and took us to the parade site. Even though the rain had slackened, the skies remained overcast. It was one of the gloomiest days ever. We climbed up on our float, and it was so wet, the water on the float seeped onto the long dress I was wearing. The entire bottom of my dress for about six to eight inches was soaked in water.

About that time, a reporter from one of the local television stations came over to ask if he could have an interview with us. He said, "What do you think the chances are for the parade?"

I said, "No *chance* at all." With God there never is an element of chance. I simply said (because God spoke to my heart), "The sun's going to come out, and there's not going to be a drop of rain on the parade."

I wish you could have seen the expression on the man's face. I was operating in a supernatural realm of faith, because I had positive knowledge that I had heard God. I was looking at the rain, the overcast sky, and momentarily (in the natural) I thought, "What did I say?" And right on television everyone heard me say, "There isn't going to be any rain on the parade."

God had given me that supernatural faith He gives to each and every one of us on those very special occasions. About 30 minutes later there was a little tiny blue place in the sky no bigger than a man's hand. With Elijah, it was just the reverse. He saw a cloud the size of a man's hand. (See 1 Kings 18:41–45.) There was a little tiny blue spot and Charles nudged me and said, "Honey, take a look at that blue spot up there; it's no bigger than a man's hand."

I said, "Hallelujah! But it's going to grow and grow and grow." Not a single drop of rain, not one single drop fell on that entire parade!

We ministered after the parade on the PTL television satellite network, and someone ran up to me and said, "There's a mute here who has never spoken in all her life. She's 28 years old."

I thought, "I'll pray for these short arms over here because that's easier." You see, I have one hundred percent faith for some things, but when it comes to a mute, I don't always have quite that much faith. Charles and I are always honest, and that's the reason I'm sharing this with you.

I went to pray for the arms and again I heard the *"still small voice"* (1 Kings 19:12) of God. He said, "Is it any harder for me to heal a mute than it is to heal a back or change the weather?" I dropped those arms and thought, "How silly! Isn't it ridiculous that we let the Devil come and tell us that we can do the little things, but not the big things?" I said, "Where is that mute?"

God had suddenly poured on me a tremendous gift of faith, and I looked at her and thought, "That's no harder than anything else." God's power is always the same. He doesn't make any differentiation in where it flows.

This faith that I had heard God was bursting within me and I said, "Stick out your tongue." She stuck out her tongue at me, so I just laid my fingers on her tongue and said, "You dumb spirit, in the name of Jesus, I have more power than you have, so come out of her right now."

For twenty-eight years she had never said a word in her entire life, and I whispered in her ear, "Say Ma-ma." And she said, "Say Ma-ma!" I was never so shocked in my life because I've never heard a mute yell that loudly when he or she got healed. She really yelled, and so I said, "Say Pa-pa." And she said, "Say Pa-pa."

Suddenly, it dawned on me that she had never heard her own lips say "Mama" before, so I pointed to her mother, a beautiful gray-haired lady standing nearby whose heart was just broken because her daughter had been mute for twenty-eight years. I pointed to her and said, "Mama."

The girl looked at her mother and said, "Mama!" For the first time in all of her life she could speak the beloved title of the woman who had taken care of her all this time! What a joyous moment that was!

How I praise God for that supernatural gift of faith that He gave me, and yet it was so simple, because I knew I had heard God speak.

I didn't work it up.

I didn't get emotional.

I just heard God and received what He had for me. *Faith is simply receiving what God has for you.* Glory!

Jesus healed a deaf mute as recorded in Mark 7:32–37. The crowd who saw the healing *"were astonished beyond measure, saying, 'He has done all things well. He makes both the deaf to hear and the mute to speak'"* (v. 37).

Doing the same things Jesus did while He was on earth for the glory of God is a twenty-first century example of possessing the mind of Christ Jesus! He's alive!

Faith is a growing process. It is not a "jump in and I've got it all" situation. It is a process of development. I believe every problem we face and subsequently overcome is a step in the right direction so that our faith will progressively be more like Jesus!

Recently, in a situation that was acted out in presumption, somebody said to me, "Give me a word of wisdom. Should we continue believing God to supply the money we need or should we go back home?"

I said, "If you have to ask me, you are trying to ride on my faith, and you can't do that; you have to operate on your own faith, because when you have to ask somebody, 'Should I continue to stand in faith?' that means your faith has wavered, and you have lost because you have not continued to believe God."

The thing that is so exciting in the story about Shadrach, Meshach, and Abed-Nego is that their faith never wavered a single, solitary bit. They didn't have to question whether or not God was going to do it; they positively knew beyond a shadow of a doubt! But notice that once their decision was made to trust God, even to giving their lives if necessary, they moved into the seemingly impossible situation with total confidence in God. They never stopped to think, "It doesn't seem to be working!" They walked into the fiery furnace of sudden death in the natural, but they kept walking.

Exercised Faith Grows

When we are developing our faith by spiritual calisthenics, each step forward strengthens our faith. When you start into some untested area of faith, keep walking and trusting God!

We have also learned that if we have not heard God clearly enough, we will go to a doctor rather than die standing on what we call faith! God speaks much about common sense along with faith. We must practice faith daily by hearing God in our normal day-to-day functions. Then our faith will grow so strong that we can hear God's direction in meeting bigger needs.

After all, faith is a gift. We don't earn it; we just walk in it by simply trusting God.

There are times when we say we believe and yet, in our hearts, we know good and well we do not. This has been one of the problems in the great faith movement that was such a big wave for about ten years. As people began to read and study and stand on the Word of God, some immature people arose who quoted faith, but in their hearts did not believe at all. God has a very secret way of looking within the very depths of our hearts to know whether or not we actually believe or whether we are just speaking words. He wants us to trust Him, and He is glorified when we do.

I think if we will just try to uncomplicate faith by taking out all the superhyped faith confessions and get back to the simplicity of believing faith, we'll be a lot better off.

Proper Timing Is Essential

Charles and I have noticed many, many times that we are forced, because we are in ministry, to make daily decisions that involve faith. We have discovered that what some people think is faith is incorrectly stepping out ahead of what God really has planned for you at that particular time. Many people have difficulties because they go beyond where God has called them at that specific time.

One of the greatest types of faith you can ever have is the knowledge that you have heard God, whether it is for a little thing or a big thing. God may be wanting a little thing in your life at this exact moment of time, and yet in the ego trap into which we often fall, we may want a bigger thing than God has planned for us at that moment. We may simply be unprepared for what we desire. It's really a question of trusting the fact that you are able to hear God in every little nitty-gritty area of your life.

Sometimes the choice we make is not a big decision requiring a lot of faith; it's just the knowledge that we are hearing from God.

We need to *listen* to God more instead of *asking* God for more.

People can often get involved in programs or projects that are a desire of the flesh, thinking, "I would like to have a big ministry. I would like to have a big church building. I would like to have this. I would like to have that." They feel that their desires are in accordance with God's will instead of listening for God to tell them what to do. If we let God tell us what to do, then we can always rest assured that we will be successful. If we have to constantly knock on the door of the throne room of God, begging, pleading, crying, and cajoling, we are actually trying to force God to do what we want. There is a very fine line in the area of faith in this respect, and it is so important for us to learn to listen to those "little things" of God. It takes just as much faith to hear God in the little things as it does in the big things.

So many times people feel that they have heard God when it is really a thought that comes from their flesh or from the Devil—I don't know which. The voice they hear causes them to say, "God told me I am going to have a big ministry and I'm going to go overseas and I'm going to speak to hundreds of thousands of people."

That same individual has never led one person on his block to the Lord.

Was that God or flesh speaking?

If we really went back and checked that thought again, we would discover in all probability that it came from the flesh and not from God. When you come right down to it, a thought like that is likely to be for your own glory rather than for the glory of God.

One of the things we have discovered is that if you listen to God, the things you accomplish will be for His glory and not for your glory. That is always a good test as to whether or not it is you or God. If you are dead to self, the desire of your heart will be to please God; if you are not dead to self, the desire of your heart will be to please self. If we check our motives, it is easy to discover what faith really is and how simple it is to operate in complete faith at all times.

"Big" faith is wanting to please God. Charles just said that, and there is a tremendous truth in that statement.

Why did Jesus have so much faith? Because He wanted to please God.

He who loves Me will be loved by My Father, and I will love him and manifest Myself to him.
—John 14:21

Six

Love

---•---

Because we possess the mind of Christ, we also possess His very heart-cry!

We possess the compassion and the love of Jesus Christ. We possess the same attributes as God because Jesus and His Father are one.

Because we are *"partakers of the divine nature"* (2 Pet. 1:4) of God, we have the mind of Christ, the nature of God, the ability of God, the character of God, the wisdom of God, and the love of God!

How should we treat those around us? How should we treat those we love? If we really do have the mind of Christ, how should we treat those we *don't* love?

We are surrounded with love! We are filled with love! We are overflowing with love! We are running over with love!

What a privilege, what a joy divine, what a glorious knowledge to know in our hearts that all these things are ours because we belong to Christ Jesus and because we possess His mind.

Probably one of the best examples in the Bible about possessing the mind of Christ concerning love is in the book of John.

The Living Bible beautifully expresses such a promise of God's love. God's love flowing into us enables us to reach out and love those who need love so badly. Jesus said, *"The one who obeys me is the one who loves me; and because he loves me, my Father will love him; and I will too, and I will reveal myself to him"* (John 14:21 TLB).

In verses 23 and 24, we read these words of Jesus, *"I will only reveal myself to those who love me and obey me. The Father will love them too, and we will come to them and live with them. Anyone who doesn't obey me doesn't love me."*

What an absolutely mind-boggling statement for us to be aware of! All we have to do is obey God, and then both Jesus and the Father will come and live in us. They will love us, love in us, and love through us. The world out there that needs so desperately to be loved is going to feel the *agape* love of God that flows through our veins simply because we are obedient to Christ Jesus.

A long time ago, I heard somebody say that God would not share His glory with anybody. However, if you read the book of John, you will see that we are the glory of God. What an absolutely extravagant statement to make. Yet it comes directly out of the Word of God!

Jesus told us in the fifteenth chapter of John that He is the vine, and His Father is the gardener (v. 1). He told us to abide in Him and let Him abide in us (v. 4).

I love what Jesus says in that chapter:

I have loved you even as the Father has loved me. Live within my love. When you obey me you are living in my love, just as I obey my Father and live in his love. I have told you this so that you will be filled with my joy. Yes, your cup of joy will overflow! I demand that you love each other as much as I love you.　　　　　　　　　　　　　　*(John 15:9–12 TLB)*

Do we fully realize what we really have in Jesus Christ? He loves us so much that He wants our cup of joy to be filled. Because I possess the mind of Christ, I am going to be filled with the joy of Jesus all of the time! What a blessing!

Possessing the mind of Christ means agreeing totally, 100 percent with everything Jesus said. If He says He came so that we could be filled with His joy, then I am going to be filled with His joy, and my cup of joy is going to absolutely overflow.

What does Jesus say about loving one another? He says, "I *demand*," which also means "I *command* you to love one another as much as I love you. I *require* you to love one another as much as I love you. I *charge* you with responsibility of loving your brother in Christ as much as I love you."

That is the mind of Christ. The desire of Jesus is that we love our brothers and sisters in Christ as much as He loved us.

Carnal Thought Produces Criticism

There are times in the Christian world when brothers and sisters begin to criticize and condemn each other. This is the carnal mind, which is the enemy of the plans and purposes of God.

When you criticize a brother or sister in Christ, you are not being obedient to Jesus, who commands us to love one another in exactly the way He loves us.

In recent years we have seen many of the large ministries get criticized and falsely accused by other Christians. This criticism is the result of operating in a carnal (fleshly) realm instead of operating in love by possessing the mind of Christ at all times.

This same criticism causes strife and division in churches!

If we see a brother or sister doing something we don't like and suddenly feel condemnation toward him or her, we should stop immediately. We ought to go to them in God's love, not in hate. We must continue in a beautiful attitude of love, saying, "Look, brother or sister, your program seems to have a problem. Let's discuss some other options. Let's pray about it." We must act in love just as Jesus did.

The *Amplified Bible* has some beautiful words on how we should feel because we possess the mind of Christ:

For the uttered words that You gave Me I have given them. And they have received and accepted [them], and have come to know positively and in reality—to believe with absolute assurance—that I came forth from Your presence. And they have believed and are convinced that You did send Me. I am praying for them. I am not praying (requesting) for the world; but for those You have given Me, for they belong to You. All Mine are Yours, and all that are Yours belong to Me; and I am glorified in (through) them—they have done Me honor, in them My glory is achieved. (John 17:8–10 AMP)

Do you realize what He said? Jesus said if we believed with absolute assurance that He came forth from the presence of God, then we are His glory! Possessing the mind of Christ means believing we are the very glory of Jesus Christ Himself!

Isn't that dangerous for hell when you know that you are the glory of God? Absolutely. If anything should make you love the almighty God even more than you love Him right now, it is the knowledge that you are the very glory of Jesus Christ!

I love what John says just a little bit further in that same chapter. Verse 16 says, *"They are not of the world, just as I am not of the world."* The first time I ever read that verse, I nearly exploded. Right along the side of my Bible I wrote, "PTL— Praise the Lord!"

Possessing the mind of Christ means that we do not have to go along with the world!

We do not have to go along with the things the world tells us to do!

We do not have to go along with our peers!

We do not have to dress as everybody else does!

We do not have to acquire the habits everybody else does!

We do not belong to this world any more than Jesus does!

If the world hates you because you do not conform to smoking, drinking, dancing, and viewing unholy movies, all I can say is, "Glory to God. That is certainly a marvelous indication that you possess the very mind of Christ."

The eighteenth verse gives us even more advice for possessing His mind. Jesus says, *"As You sent Me into the world, I also have sent them into the world."*

If we possess the mind of Christ, then we are going to know that we are sent into the world—maybe not in the international sense, but in the sense of our own little individual world that includes our family, our children, our parents, our brothers and sisters. We are sent into *our* world to share the good news about Jesus Christ.

Possessing the mind of Christ is a subject that has no beginning or ending. You can find Jesus in every book in the Bible, whether it is the Old Testament or the New Testament. Every thought of Jesus was saturated with and soaked in God's love for people. We will also be saturated with and soaked in the same love for people if we possess the mind of Christ. Think love! God's love!

The joy of the LORD is your strength.
—Nehemiah 8:10

Seven

Joy

Joy is a priceless and invaluable commodity available to the Christian. Not something that can be bought or sold, but a gift available to every born-again believer from the Lord Jesus Christ!

My own joy started the day I was saved. When I realized that all my sins were forgiven, I was so completely overwhelmed with thanksgiving that my joy just bubbled up and overflowed. What an explosive thought—my sins were forgiven, all of them! I literally wallowed in the glory of that moment for weeks, and then realized that something more had to be done to keep that "up" level going strong all the time!

If we want that eternal spring of joy welling up and bubbling over in us at all times, we need to get into the Word of God for a spiritual feast. We must take big bites and continue chewing until our souls are fat. The real, lasting, genuine joy never comes until we are spiritually fat!

Jesus had a lot to say about joy, and since we possess His mind, we need to agree with Him in every area.

*If you keep My commandments, you will abide in My love,
just as I have kept My Father's commandments and abide in
His love. These things I have spoken to you, that My joy may
remain in you, and that your joy may be full. (John 15:10–11)*

This particular Scripture explains better than any other
how Jesus feels about joy. He had to possess joy, or Jesus
would not have said in that last verse, *"**My** joy may remain in
you"* (emphasis added). He expected that we would have joy
and gladness, or He would not have said, *"And that **your** joy
may be full"* (emphasis added).

Jesus said His joy and delight would remain in us, and
our joy would be full, full, full! Not just a partial cup of joy,
but one that is full measure, complete and overflowing! All of
this is ours if we will just stay vitally united with Him at all
times. He wants us to have the absolute maximum of joy in
our lives at all times. Glory!

Joy Releases Strength

Charles and I have often been asked how we maintain the
hectic, grueling schedule we keep all the time. Nehemiah 8:10
gives the answer, *"The joy of the LORD is your strength!"*

Marilyn Hickey was talking to us recently after we had
returned from a super long trip, and she said, "The joy of the
Lord is your total strength, isn't it? You'd never be able to
accomplish what you do if you didn't absorb your strength
from the joy of the Lord!"

Another friend said about us, "They refuse to let anyone or
anything steal their joy." Think about that for a moment. If you
allow circumstances or people, or yourself (by negative thinking about yourself) to take your attention away from God and

service to others, you will find yourself becoming discouraged, discontent, depressed, worried, uptight, or having some other incorrect, selfish attitude come into your heart.

If you want something to sap your strength fast, let that happen to you! But if you want to keep strong and healthy, let the joy of the Lord be your strength!

When Jesus told His disciples that He would be going away, but that He would send the Comforter to them, He knew they did not know understand His words. He knew they were questioning among themselves and that

> *they wanted to ask him so he said, "Are you asking yourselves what I mean? The world will greatly rejoice over what is going to happen to me, and you will weep. But your weeping shall suddenly be turned to wonderful joy [when you see me again]. It will be the same joy as that of a woman in labor when her child is born—her anguish gives place to rapturous joy and the pain is forgotten."* (John 16:19–21 TLB)

If you are a mother, you can remember when you had your baby. Do you often recall how much it hurt? No, we seldom do. Mothers know how painful childbirth can be, and yet when you see that darling little boy or girl God gave to you, your anguish gives way to rapturous joy, and the pain is forgotten. I will never forget the first thing I said to the doctor after my son Tom was born. His daddy was overseas fighting for the Navy, and I wanted a brown-eyed boy that looked just like his daddy. The nurse had said to me, "Don't scream until the last pain, because remember each one is going to be worse than the one before," so when the last one got there, I was waiting for the next one that never came! Then came the good news after all the bad pains. "It's a big boy!"

I said, "My cup runneth over—let me kiss him!"

My cup of joy was overflowing all over the place. I wasn't even a Christian, but in that moment when birth actually took place, I instantly forgot all the pain, and all I could think about was how I wanted to kiss that little bundle of humanity God had given to me. Just as the Scripture had said, *"Her anguish gives place to rapturous joy and the pain is forgotten"* (John 16:21 TLB).

Jesus said, *"You have sorrow now, but I will see you again and then you will rejoice; and no one can rob you of that joy"* (v. 22 TLB). *"No one can rob you of that joy"*! Beloved, don't you ever let anybody take that joy out of your life. The Devil will do his best to rob you of every bit of your Christian joy, but remember, it's Jesus' joy that you have!

Continuing with John 16:23–24, we read:

And in that day you will ask Me nothing. Most assuredly, I say to you, whatever you ask the Father in My name He will give you. Until now you have asked nothing in My name. Ask, and you will receive, that your joy may be full.

Because we possess the mind of Christ, we need to agree with Him in every single area, and joy is one area that He talked a lot about. Christians should never run around with long faces, but we should be full of the joy of the Lord at all times. Even right now, I pray for such a big cupful of joy for you that you will instantly be bubbling over with the joy of the Lord.

Were you a "sweet" sinner or a "nasty" one? In our family we always say that Charles was the "sweet" sinner and I was the "nasty" one, but the end result would have been the same for both of us. Praise God, the "now" result is exactly the same for each of us. We are constantly overflowing with the joy of the Lord. All you have to do to receive joy into your life is to remember when you were born again, your sins were all forgiven and they were buried in the deepest sea—never to be remembered again! (See Psalm 103:12.) If that doesn't make you run over with the joy of the Lord, nothing will! Just to know that your sins are gone, gone, gone is enough to bring joy to the world's unhappiest person!

Jesus wants us to have an everlasting supply of joy and gives us the conditions to have that never-ending supply. In John 15:7, He says, *"If you abide in Me, and My words abide in you, you will ask what you desire, and it shall be done for you."* If you will give some extra consideration to that Scripture and meditate upon it, you will discover something that should make you jump for joy. All you have to do is "abide" in Him, and then whatever you ask will be done for you. This might seem strange that you can just ask anything and it will be done for you, but we need to remember that when you "abide" in Him or "go into" Him, your desires will be exactly the same as His desires. That's why He gives us so much leeway to *"ask what you desire."*

The word *joy* is used 199 times in the Bible, so it didn't just slip in there accidentally. The parable of the talents is an exciting story about Jesus speaking joy into people who were obedient to Him. When the man returned with five additional talents on top of the original five, Jesus spoke words to him that should encourage anyone who is not full of the joy of the Lord. Jesus wants us to be joyful. *"Well done, good and faithful servant; you were faithful over a few things, I will make you ruler over many things. Enter into the **joy** of your Lord"* (Matt. 25:21, emphasis added).

94

Obedience Brings Joy

Being obedient gives us the privilege of entering into the joy of the Lord. Jesus must have felt this was a great reward for him to enter into the most delightful of all joys, the joy of the Lord!

"The kingdom of God is not eating and drinking, but righteousness and peace and joy in the Holy Spirit" (Rom. 14:17). If we're living in the kingdom of God, then we have not only righteousness and peace, but also joy, joy, joy in the Holy Spirit!

"Jesus joy" cannot be erased, obliterated, canceled out, or blotted out by anyone but ourselves. Jesus wants you to have joy in your heart at all times because the greatest help in the time of problems and tribulations is that everlasting joy that Jesus puts into the hearts of those who love Him and are obedient to Him.

Anyone in ministry is subject to problems. Problems arise frequently. The single quality that has taken Charles and me through everything that has come up is that constant joy in our hearts, indelibly stamped there by the Master Himself, when He gave us salvation.

The problems of the world seem dim in comparison to the joy of knowing that Jesus Christ lives in and through you.

Look at all the joy expressed in Psalm 5:11–12:

But let all those rejoice who put their trust in You;
(Let's rejoice, rejoice, rejoice!)
Let them ever shout for joy,
(We don't have to be silent; we can even shout and shout and shout!)
because You defend them; let those also who love Your name

be joyful in You.
(I love your name, I love your name, I love your name,
so I cannot be anything but joyful, Lord!)
For You, O LORD, will bless the righteous;
(Thank you, Lord, thank you, Lord, for blessing me!)
with favor You will surround him as with a shield.

Glory to God, we're surrounded with a shield because God's favor is upon us; therefore, "I've got the joy, joy, joy, joy down in my heart!" Glory!

*When you have done all those things which you are
commanded, say, "We are unprofitable servants.
We have done what was our duty to do."
—Luke 17:10*

Eight

The Master–Slave Relationship

———•———

The word *servant* comes from the Greek word *doulos,* which has a beautiful meaning. A *doulos* is a person who gives himself wholly to another's will. The dictionary describes a servant as "a slave," or "a person ardently devoted to another or to a cause or creed." That is exactly the way Jesus wants us to be—totally submissive to His will, giving ourselves completely to Him, utterly laying aside our own lives and desires just to do His will.

Jesus was a servant of God. He became a man in order to be a servant of God. Jesus gave Himself totally to God's will. We need to give ourselves totally to His will, also. We should be so committed to the cause of Jesus Christ that it overwhelms us and totally dominates our every thought.

Once we can truly understand the "slave" relationship we have with the Lord Jesus Christ, we will experience more freedom in our lives than we have ever known before.

Paul said a tremendous thing in the second chapter of Galatians, verse 20:

I have been crucified with Christ; it is no longer I who live, but Christ lives in me; and the life which I now live in the flesh I live by faith in the Son of God, who loved me and gave Himself for me.

When we get that Scripture into our hearts, into our minds, and into our spirits, we will possess the "servant" mind of Christ. Dying to self is one of the most important principles we will ever learn when we possess the mind of Christ. Jesus had to die to self in order to please His Father, and we have to die to self in order to be able to please God and Jesus.

There is a tremendous message to be gained by the body of Christ in really learning how to think as Jesus thought. In the seventeenth chapter of Luke, Jesus talked about having faith as a mustard seed. He said,

If you have faith as a mustard seed, you can say to this mulberry tree, "Be pulled up by the roots and be planted in the sea," and it would obey you. And which of you, having a servant plowing or tending sheep, will say to him when he has come in from the field, "Come at once and sit down to eat"? But will he not rather say to him, "Prepare something for my supper, and gird yourself and serve me till I have eaten and drunk, and afterward you will eat and drink"? Does he thank that servant because he did the things that were commanded him? I think not. So likewise you, when you have done all those things which you are commanded, say, "We are unprofitable servants. We have done what was our duty to do."
(Luke 17:6–10)

Jesus was trying to convince us that there is a master–slave relationship between us and God. We rebel against being a slave, and yet the slave is the one who receives the unmerited grace, the unmerited favor, and the blessings of God if he is willing to put himself in a position of servitude. If we are willing to completely die to our own desires, our own wills, and want nothing except the will of God, then we will be that perfect servant exactly like Jesus.

My twentieth-century translation of what He said is, "Don't come in and order the boss around." The servant does not come in and put his feet under the table and say, "Boss, you serve me."

Don't fall into the very real trap of believing that we can command God to do things. Jesus is saying to us, "If you'll just be the servant, then God will say to you, 'Well done, good and faithful servant.'"

When we can accept that owner–slave relationship and be so committed to God and Jesus that we have no personal desires of our own, we can begin to operate exactly as God wants us to and receive all the blessings God has waiting for us.

Is it really possible for us to totally die to self and deny fleshly desires in today's world with all the outside interference and competition from the things of the Devil? Yes!

No Vacation Needed Here

I firmly believe that Charles and I are normal Christians. Neither of us has any desire whatsoever to do anything except what God has called us to do. We work 365 days out of every year. You might ask if we work on Sundays. Yes, if you want to call it work. We minister over half of the year in meetings around the world, in addition to our regular office responsibilities and writing books. The reason we have such tremendous joy is because we crucified all the desires we had in our lives when we became totally committed to God.

Charles used to love vacations before we were married. He would drive thousands of miles every year sightseeing, picking up all kinds of souvenirs, and looking for ways to enjoy the things of this world. There's nothing wrong with that, but God has replaced seeking pleasure with a burning zeal to do His work. God still lets us see His beautiful creation while we do His work.

I used to do the same thing. I'd love to go on vacation and see all the sights. I remember riding down to the bottom of the Grand Canyon on a mule. When I got back up, my legs were so sore I thought I wasn't going to be able to walk for a week.

I thought, "Wow, this is really fun."

Since Charles and I made a total commitment of our lives to God, we have never had a vacation.

People often ask, "When are you going to take your vacation?"

We say, "Never." People take a vacation to get away from everything. I don't want to get away from anything. The thing that makes me the happiest is ministering unto the Lord and doing the things He has called us to do.

Because we are involved in doing the Lord's work twenty-four hours a day, seven days a week, we don't need a vacation.

There isn't a vacation you could give us any place in the world that would compare with our having a miracle service.

Take a vacation? No, thank you. I want to be doing the things of God every second of my life. That's my first love.

Now you might say, "How do I get to the point when I will feel that same way? I have to get up every morning at 6:00 and go to work collecting garbage for the city where I live. This is my income source; this is my job. Truthfully, I can't stand my job, but I have to get up and do it. You mean to tell me you don't think I ought to take a vacation?"

Your circumstances are different from ours. You quite possibly do need a vacation to get away from what you are doing in the secular world. I would certainly recommend a retreat or convention where you can rest in the Lord and develop spiritually among other believers during your one or two weeks' vacation. There are many fantastic Christian retreats where whole families enjoy these benefits in a Christian atmosphere.

When we worked in our secular jobs, we chose to use our evenings and weekends to win people to Jesus, so even then we didn't need a vacation.

New priorities replaced old ones.

Submission Must Be Willing

Foot washing, if it were practiced today, would make more of us more aware of what the servant–master, owner–slave relationship truly is.

In the thirteenth chapter of John, we find an extremely fascinating story of Jesus becoming a slave.

He got up from the supper table, took off his robe, wrapped a towel around his loins, poured water into a basin, and began

to wash the disciples' feet and to wipe them with the towel he
had around him. *(John 13:4–5 TLB)*

Peter immediately became indignant and told Jesus that He certainly shouldn't be washing the feet of the disciples. Peter told Jesus he wasn't going to let Him wash his feet, but Jesus said if He did not, then he could not be a *"partner"* (v. 8 TLB) with Him.

Jesus utterly amazed His disciples when He knelt down and washed their feet. At that moment He was the epitome of servanthood!

To me this is the most beautiful of all the ordinances because I had such a unique experience the first time I ever participated in a foot-washing service. I could not believe anyone in the twentieth century would wash someone else's feet. My pastor merely teased me and said, "Come and see."

I came, I saw, and I experienced something beyond compare where love is concerned!

When you kneel down to wash someone's feet, you become a total slave to that person. The Master completely humbled Himself when He became a servant. If only we could see that truth in our own lives! If we would be willing to do anything and everything God calls us to do and Jesus tells us in the Word, we would be able to climb to heights beyond our greatest dreams.

Even at this very moment as I sit writing this book, I remember what I felt the first time I ever washed somebody else's feet. I felt God was so close I could have reached up and wrapped my arms around Him. I was so completely enveloped in His love and so totally engulfed in His presence that it was almost equal to an out-of-body experience.

The same love Jesus felt for His disciples flowed through me as I washed the tiny little feet of my pastor's wife.

A foot-washing service conducted under proper circumstances in every church or denomination could be one of the greatest things that could ever happen to the body of Christ. When you wash someone else's feet, you will feel the very servanthood of Jesus as He washed the disciples' feet.

A long time ago I heard a testimony of a very brilliant young Jewish man who had gone around the world seeking the answer to life. He was picked up in Switzerland and was discussing the problems and futility of life when the little old man who gave him a ride touched his hand and said, "Men ought to wash other men's feet!" It was said with so much love that it was as though his heart had exploded. That simple little statement caused the Jewish young man to accept Jesus as his personal Messiah.

One year at our Bible school, as I was teaching on the book of John, I shared with the students my experiences in connection with a foot-washing ceremony, and the Spirit of God spoke to me and said to have a foot-washing service the next day for all the students.

We quickly made the arrangements, and the next morning I told them what we were going to do. Many of the students were unwilling to participate, so we made it very plain that it was a decision on their part because they would not be forced to participate.

We started with singing in two separate circles. Charles had the men, and I ministered to the women. We sang, "Oh, How I Love Jesus," and other similar songs. Pretty soon we noticed other students coming forward to sit in one of the circles. Before we finished, not only had all the students participated, but they had even gone over into our office and told our staff what was happening. Many of the staff participated, too! It was a genuine experience of becoming a servant.

"Men ought to wash other men's feet!"

But we all, with unveiled face, beholding as in a mirror the glory of the Lord, are being transformed into the same image from glory to glory, just as by the Spirit of the Lord.
—2 Corinthians 3:18

Nine

The Glory of God

Did Jesus believe in the glory of God? In John 11:39 we observe Jesus talking to Martha, the sister of Mary and Lazarus.

Lazarus had just died. Martha thought Jesus had fiddle-faddled around getting there. Thinking Jesus had let her brother die and then just "lie there" all that time, was really heartbreaking to Martha.

Jesus spoke and said, *"Take away the stone"* (v. 39).

Martha replied, *"Lord, by this time there is a stench, for he has been dead four days"* (v. 39).

In the natural, Martha was right. Lazarus probably didn't smell very good by that time. She was totally controlled by her senses.

Let's look at this with the mind of Christ. If we live in the supernatural world, then we ought to be moved by the supernatural and not by our senses. When you are born again by the Spirit of God, your spirit takes on an eternal characteristic. You actually become a supernatural person in your spirit.

You are still a physical being. You are still walking on this earth, but your spirit becomes supernatural because your spirit has been born again by the Spirit of God.

We are *in* the world, but we are *"not of the world"* (John 17:14, 16, emphasis added). Our spirits live in the supernatural realm.

If we really believe that, then what are we going to do? We are going to operate, walk, and live in the supernatural glory of God at all times. Why? Because we are not the earthly beings we were before we got saved.

You can operate in the supernatural realm to such a degree that you trust God more than you have ever trusted Him in your entire life. That's living in the supernatural realm and not in the sense realm.

How do we operate, walk, and live in the supernatural realm? By utilizing the mind of Christ. He lives within us. He walks where we walk. He talks when we talk. In every situation, stop and ask this simple question: "If Jesus were standing here right now, what would He say? What would He do?"

Since Jesus is living inside of every born-again believer, He is living within you. Once your spirit catches hold of the fact that He is always there to guide you, you can always do what He would do in every situation. You will live in the supernatural realm in which He is living today.

Let's go back to Martha for a moment. Obviously, she was totally hung up on the natural circumstances.

Jesus said to Martha, *"Did I not say to you that if you would believe you would see the glory of God?"* (v. 40).

Want to See His Glory?

The only way you'll ever see the glory of God is to just believe. *Believe* is such a beautiful word! When you get to the point where you really believe in the glory of God and the supernatural, you will walk closer to God than ever before. You will then walk in the supernatural at all times.

Jesus said, *"Did I not say to you that if you would believe you would see the glory of God?"* (John 11:40).

Just believe, and you will see the glory of God! I think the desire of every Christian is to see the glory of God and to walk in His presence.

Recently, I received a computer printout on the word *glory.* I have gone through my *Amplified Bible* marking the words *glory* and *glorified* every time I came across them. Each time I open my Bible to a marked page, I know that the word *glory* is there. If there were several *glory*s on the page, I even put a mark at the top of the page. That mark tells me "Wow, this page is a goodie!"

If you want people to see the glory of God, just digest a few choice morsels from these particular pages. Get a concordance and go through your Bible marking the word *glory* each time you find it.

One of the verses I love the most about *glory* is Numbers 14:21, which says, *"But truly, as I live, all the earth shall be filled with the glory of the LORD."*

Can you imagine if the whole world were filled with believers? Can you imagine the glory of God that we would be walking in? God's glory dims when people don't believe. As a matter of fact, unbelievers don't get to see the glory of God, except on very rare occasions.

Can you just imagine if we were walled in with 1,000 or 10,000 or 50,000 real believers? Do you have any idea of the glory of God that would be present? We would be like Moses. We would have to go into the *"cleft of the rock"* (Exod. 33:22). God would have to put His hand over us because we couldn't stand to see the full force of His glory.

A First Peek at Glory

Charles and I have been so blessed to be able to have seen the glory of God. The first time was quite some time ago in Redding, California, in the Civic Center.

I almost missed what happened because I really didn't know what it was. I thought the place was just suddenly getting foggy.

But something in my spirit leaped, and I knew it was the supernatural presence and the power of God. It was just as if waves of the ocean had started to rush in over the back of the auditorium.

This particular auditorium is made like a bowl with seats that go up the back, not on the sides. Just like a wave of the sea, a big cloud came crashing over the seats and rolled to the floor level. The waves continued until they covered everyone in that auditorium.

When you see the glory cloud of God, something definitely happens inside of you. When the glory is present and accepted, miracles happen with a magnitude difficult for the natural man to comprehend.

The glory of God rolled in that day in Redding, California. What an exciting time that was! When the glory of God touches people, they are going to be changed either spiritually or physically. I really believe it's God's will that they are changed both ways.

A bus came in that day from a place called Paradise, California. Of the people on the bus, fifty percent were sick and fifty percent came because they enjoyed attending miracle services. Every sick person on that bus without a single exception was healed by the power of God.

Glory Always Produces Change

When you sit in the glory of God and you openly receive the glory of God, something is going to happen to you. You can't sit in the presence and the glory of God and come out of it exactly the same. Charles and I have never been the same from that day when the Shechinah glory of God rolled in all over that auditorium.

The testimonies are still mind boggling!

Three little cross-eyed children were healed by the power of God.

A lady who had traveled all the way from Boise, Idaho, had been on the bus the entire day and night before. She was in such agony with rheumatoid arthritis that she could hardly walk, talk, or speak. As she sat under the glory of God, she was instantly and totally healed by the power of God without anybody praying for her. Without anybody laying hands on her or doing anything, she got up and began to dance. Hallelujah!

Tremendous healings took place that day.

Why? Because somebody laid hands on them? No. When you just sit in the glory of God and feel the presence of God encompassing you, a spiritual and physical change will happen on the inside of you. I just love meetings where the glory of God covers every single person, going into all the little cracks, crevices, and corners.

If you can just get your spirit man so in tune with the Word of God, you will believe in the anointing of God, you will believe in the glory of God, and you will see things you have never seen in your entire life.

Angels Come with the Glory Cloud

I am excited because more and more people are reporting to us that they are seeing angels. Is that because God has more and more angels to send to earth today?

No. Angels don't reproduce themselves. There are no more angels today than there were 2,000 years ago. Angels are protecting you and working with you wherever you go. (See Revelation 19:10.)

God stationed an angel with us in Abilene, Texas, in 1978. He explained to us, "That angel is a special warrior angel that I have sent to protect you from the fiery darts of the Devil until Jesus Christ comes back again."

Wherever Charles and I go, we know we are protected by a giant warrior angel whom we often see. He gives us an extra feeling of security at all times.

Did Jesus believe in the glory of God? Jesus believed in His Father's glory or He would never have said to Martha,

*"If you would **believe**, you would see the glory of God"* (John 11:40, emphasis added).

That was a promise He was making to Martha. He was telling her that the Father loved her so much that He was going to let her get a little sample of the glory of God.

God loves us so much that He wants us to see His glory, too.

Oh, beloved, just believe, and He will open your spiritual eyes to His glorious supernatural world.

We possess the mind of Christ! Are we going to be scoffers? Are we going to be scorners?

Are we going to say, "I don't believe that is what God is doing today. I don't believe God is sending fire into services. I don't believe God is sending His glory cloud."

Well, have I got news for you! If Jesus said it, Jesus believed it, and I'm going to believe it, too. I am looking for more and more of the supernatural to be obvious to the believers.

Let me put in a little word of caution right here. The Bible says, *"And these signs will follow those who believe"* (Mark 16:17).

Don't run after signs and wonders—let the signs and wonders run after you. Then when they happen, you will enjoy them even more!

The Vision of Jesus

At our camp meeting in 1983, which was entitled "A Supernatural Spree," we were worshipping God on a Saturday afternoon. During praise and worship is when you are likely to really see the supernatural power of God displayed.

Directly behind me appeared a huge white cloud. It was so thick it looked like it actually had substance. I felt as though I could reach out, touch it, and get a handful. It was so white it looked like Marshmallow Creme.

I thought "Wow, that's really neat up there, isn't it?"

I did not yet have any idea what was going to happen. This cloud mushroomed just exactly the way a thunderhead looks in the sky. They are always so super white with that mushroom shape on top. This cloud was also super white, and it was mammoth.

As I watched, I thought, "Oh, the glory of God!"

My spirit was stirred. You cannot evaluate the manifestation of His presence by whether or not you shake, vibrate, or get goose pimples that are ten feet high. People experience the presence of God in different ways.

The presence of God entered the auditorium in a new and different way than I had seen before. I watched. If I were asked to describe what the cloud looked like up there, I would have to say it looked like a cocoon.

Out of the center appeared the Lord Jesus Christ in all of His glory and His power and His majesty. My heart exploded within me.

Once before Jesus appeared to me in person. We were in a meeting in a little town of Alexandria, Indiana, several years ago.

As Jesus sat down beside me, He said, "The anointing is on Charles tonight, and he is to speak. You are to listen."

When Jesus appears to you in person, it affects your whole life. You will have an anchor point in your life like never before. You will never again doubt the reality of God. You will never again doubt the call of God.

Jesus appears as a blessing from God and usually as a tremendous surprise. Don't believe that you can ever imagine that Jesus is right here, and thus see Him. It won't do you a bit of good.

I was so overcome with the presence of God, I just stood there as if I had been struck dumb and stared at Jesus as He appeared on the stage just a few feet away from me. All I knew was that I was basking in the glory of God.

Then Jesus disappeared into the cloud.

"Oh, Jesus," I wanted to cry out. "Don't go away! Don't go away! Come back! Come back! Come back!"

However, I remained silent because the service was still going on.

I was thinking, "How many other people are seeing exactly the same thing I'm seeing?"

I wanted everybody to see Him.

Suddenly, He appeared again.

Excitement coursed through me again. How long He stayed visible I really don't know. When you are seeing in the Spirit, time tends to stand still. What seemed like twelve to fifteen minutes could actually have been a matter of a few seconds. I certainly didn't think about looking at my watch. I didn't think about looking at anything other than Him.

All I was thinking about was Jesus. I was totally caught up into the glory of God. Coming and going in and out of the cloud, He appeared several times.

Suddenly, God spoke, "That's the way I want you to be. I want you to be so lost in Him that when people see you, all they will see is the glory of God. All they will see is My glory."

Many times since that day, I have pondered why God allowed such a supernatural manifestation of His presence. The reality of what God was saying came to me very vividly.

> *Jesus spoke these words, lifted up His eyes to heaven, and said: "Father, the hour has come. Glorify Your Son, that Your Son also may glorify You, as You have given Him authority over all flesh, that He should give eternal life to as many as You have given Him. And this is eternal life, that they may know You, the only true God, and Jesus Christ whom You have sent. I have glorified You on the earth. I have finished the work which You have given Me to do. And now, O Father, glorify Me together with Yourself, with the glory which I had with You before the world was."*   *(John 17:1–5)*

He was saying, "Father, while I was down here on the earth, I was walking with all that glory. Now, My work is finished. Glorify Me together with Yourself with all the glory that I had with You before the world began. Father, do this so they will know You!"

> *I have manifested Your name to the men whom You have given Me out of the world. They were Yours, You gave them to Me, and they have kept Your word. Now they have known that all things which You have given Me are from You. For I have given to them the words which You have given Me;*

*and they have received them, and have known surely that I
came forth from You; and they have believed that You sent Me.
(John 17:6–8)*

Jesus was praying. He was saying, "Oh, Father, I pray
for those You have given Me. I don't pray that You will take
them out of the world, but that You will protect them from the
Evil One. I'm praying for those You have given Me for they
belong to You. I want them to be in heaven with You and Me,
and I want them to see My glory, which You have given Me,
because they are My glory."

*And the glory which You gave Me I have given them, that they
may be one just as We are one: I in them, and You in Me;
that they may be made perfect in one, and that the world may
know that You have sent Me, and have loved them as You have
loved Me.   (John 17:22–23)*

Do you understand what He said? Jesus is glorified in you
and in me. *The Living Bible* says, *"They are my glory!"* (v. 10).

God's Glorious Desire

Think back to what I shared about our camp meeting. Do
you remember what God said?

He said, "I want you to be so in Him, I want you to abide
so in Him, that when people look at you, they will not be
able to see you in the flesh. All they will be able to see is My
glory."

When God gives you a revelation, you're going to have to
sit down and think about it. You're going to have to get
back in the Word and say, "God, show me in the Bible the

message You were trying to give me that day when Jesus appeared."

I began to go back over this seventeenth chapter of John. It became so real to me that God wants us to be so abiding in Him, so "going into Him" that when people look at us, when they look at you, when they look at me, all they're going to be able to see is the Lord Jesus Christ.

He is the glory of God, so what are they going to see when they look at you and me?

They are going to see only the glory of God.

They are going to see the presence of God surrounding you.

They are going to see an aura of holiness around you as they have never seen before.

Do you know what this is going to do to the sinner in this end time? These are the times God was speaking about when He said, "Put in the sickle. Just put in the sickle." (See Joel 3:13.)

The fields are so *"white for harvest"* (John 4:35) that you don't have to spend time talking to people for hours about Jesus. Let the glory of God be so seen upon you that your presence, your very presence, will convict the sinner.

God has so much to offer if we just realize that all He wants is a total commitment. No person with a sin-stained life is ever going to see the glory of God. God is looking for a people who are willing to make a total commitment of their lives to love Him with their minds, their hearts, their bodies, and their souls. He is looking for a people who are not interested in the things of the world, but only in the things of God.

He's saying, "Get the sin out of your life; get anything out of your life that keeps you from being a part of Me." Does Jesus believe that? Yes! Jesus is coming back for a bride without a single spot or wrinkle or blemish, and these are the days when God is speaking to the body of Christ about really cleaning up their lives.

God is saying to the body of Christ, "Are you spending all the time you should in reading My Word? Are you spending all the time you should in communicating with Me? Are you spending all the time you should winning people to Jesus?" He says that when you get yourself on that level, that's when He will be able to show you His glory.

Jesus said,

Make them pure and holy through teaching them your words of truth. As you sent me into the world, I am sending them into the world, and I consecrate myself to meet their need for growth in truth and holiness.   *(John 17:17–19 TLB)*

Jesus committed His life to meet our need for growth not only in truth, but also in holiness. Let us never let Him down.

Then He said,

I am not praying for these alone but also for the future believers who will come to me because of the testimony of these. My prayer for all of them is that they will be of one heart and mind, just as you and I are, Father—that just as you are in me and I am in you, so they will be in us, and the world will believe you sent me.   *(John 17:20–21 TLB)*

Do you remember what I said that God told me? He said, "I want you to be so in Him, I want you to be one with Him,

I want you to be so in Jesus that when people look at you, all they will be able to think about is the Lord Jesus Christ, and the power of conviction will fall over them."

I can hardly wait until the day when God's saints just march down the street and sinners fall down and cry out, "God, save me!"

Do you think that is far-fetched? No, that is not, because that is exactly what God is doing in these end times. You are going to see more and more Christians walking in the glory of God with the joy of the Lord all over them. You are going to be able to see them shining in His glory. You will be able to pick them out of a crowd of a thousand people.

Jesus has separated us and set us apart from the things of the world, and what the world is enjoying. If we get into the Word of God, love God, believe God, and commit our lives to Him, we won't be interested in doing any of the carnal things of the world.

He closes that wonderful chapter in John with some glorious, inspiring promises to you and to me in the twentieth century.

> *I have given them the glory you gave me—the glorious unity of being one, as we are—I in them and you in me, all being perfected into one—so that the world will know you sent me and will understand that you love them as much as you love me. Father, I want them with me—these you've given me—so that they can see my glory. You gave me the glory because you loved me before the world began! O righteous Father, the world doesn't know you, but I do; and these disciples know you sent me. And I have revealed you to them, and will keep on revealing you so that the mighty love you have for me may be in them, and I in them.* (John 17:22–26 TLB)

Jesus lives in us!

We possess the mind of Christ!

We think the thoughts of Jesus!

We say the words Jesus said! He said the glory God had given Him, He gave to us. Let us walk in the presence of God because Jesus lives in us and we possess His mind!

He's coming back for a bride without a single spot, wrinkle, or blemish. Let's be excited about being a part of that bride and walk in the glory of God!

As for me and my house, we're going to walk in the glory of God all the days of our lives. Join us!

More Glory

At a meeting in Decatur, Illinois, on the final night of a convention, the glory cloud of God filled the entire place like a thin cloud of smoke, angels were more numerous than people, and a solid blanket of blue flame covered the entire audience.

Then God spoke, "Which is the hottest, the yellow flame, the orange flame, or the blue flame? The blue flame. Therefore, I have sent my hottest fire to burn out the sin in your life because I have called this group to a special ministry."

A second word from the Lord immediately followed, which concerned getting sin out of lives and receiving a real baptism with fire.

Reports came to us later that we were the only ones who slept that night. The entire 1,500 people who were present were so aware of the glory of God that they could only praise and worship Him who had sent it all night long! It's just as Jesus said, *"If you* [will only] *believe you* [will] *see the glory of God"* (John 11:40)!

David said his heart cried out for God. He was so excited when he saw the ark of the covenant coming back that he had to dance before the Lord. He said, *"I am willing to act like a fool in order to show my joy in the Lord"* (2 Sam. 6:21 TLB). He said this because the ark of the covenant contained the glory of God. David was a man after God's own heart (1 Sam. 13:14; Acts 13:22), and he wanted to see the glory of God at all times. So do I!

I have a feeling that the New Testament church was one of the most exciting churches in world history. They certainly didn't sit there like bumps on a log. I believe that every time they got together they had a fantastic, wingding time.

I believe they worshipped God. I believe they sang, clapped their hands, and jumped around rejoicing because they were in the kingdom of God. I also believe that if you went to church and said, "I have a pain," every hand in the church would be on top of your head in nothing flat, and everyone would be asking God for a miracle. That's why the Bible records so many miracles that happened when the disciples just walked by and their shadow fell upon people. (See Acts 5:15.) When the disciples touched the sick, those who had been ill were instantly healed because the glory of God was there!

Around the beginning of the twentieth century, there was a tremendous wave released as God mightily poured out His Spirit. People at that time worshipped God with their hands up in the air. "Praise God, praise God, Hallelujah!" They really had fun in church because they believed that church was the most exciting place in the world. But what happens to a lot of people? We get formal after we have gone to church for a while.

Did you ever take a look at new converts? They absolutely act like they don't have a bit of sense in their head. They want to run around and tell everybody about Jesus.

I remember in my own life that I practically beat people over the head when I first got saved because I had to share with everyone what a man named Jesus had done in my life. I was about as wild as you could get. I am still the same way!

The same thing happens when we receive the baptism with the Holy Spirit. We pray in tongues all night long. We get so excited we can't go to sleep, and we think the fervor will never wear off and hope it doesn't.

Drifting Is Unnecessary

The peculiar thing is, the same thing happens in your love affair with God as happens to many married couples. They are madly in love with each other when they get married and can't stand to be apart, but before long they can't stand to be together!

Our love affair with God and our love affair with our husband or wife are alike in many ways! Both of them need to be nurtured. We need to spend a lot of time and attention with each relationship if we want to get the most out of each one. Many times after people have been married for several years, they don't sit nearly as close to each other. They don't hold hands the way they used to hold hands. They don't put their arms around each other. Suddenly, love gets a little bit cooler and a little bit cooler and a little bit cooler. What happened to the glory of marriage?

It should never be that way. We should love each other more, not less. Every day that we are married, every single day that we are married, we ought to love God and our spouse more than we did the day before. Marriage is the most exciting institution God ever invented. God laid down the guidelines for it. It's exciting because He wants us to be happy. God does not want us to be unhappy, but it is when we don't do our part, don't nurture, protect, water, and fertilize our love, that marriage begins to wither and die.

Charles and I have been married many, many years, and I love my husband in a much wilder way than I did when we were first married. Why? Because each of us does everything we can to please the other one and to make each other happy. That is why our love continues to grow. I'll give you the secret of our marriage: Jesus is the center of our home, the center of our marriage, and the center of each of our lives. I believe that is the only thing that will keep your marriage relationship as exciting as it should be.

Many people do exactly the same thing with God. They get saved and say, "Glory to God, Hallelujah, I'm saved. I'm saved, and all my sins have been forgiven and forgotten. Praise God, praise God!" They begin to walk in the glory of God for a while, and slowly something happens. They get involved in the things of the world.

That song that says, "Turn your eyes upon Jesus, look full in His wonderful face, and the things of this earth will grow strangely dim, in the light of His glory and grace," is certainly a good song about the glory of God. People don't always continue to look in the face of Jesus, so the things of this world grow strangely bright. As they begin looking in the face of the Devil, the things of the world become far more important than the things of God.

Suddenly, their love affair with God and Jesus, which burned so brightly and caused them to walk in His glory, has grown lukewarm. There is nothing in the world more disheartening than a love affair that is lukewarm or a relationship with Jesus Christ that is lukewarm.

Turn Up the Flame

The ultimate glory of God is never visible until the flame is turned up all the way. I have often said that if I were ever going to be lukewarm I'd rather be a wild sinner instead, because the most miserable person in the world is one who knows God, but has walked away from His truth and His glory.

At a meeting in Saskatoon, Saskatchewan, Canada, God did a supernatural miracle to show His glory. People were slain by the power of God by the hundreds. God did it supernaturally because the ones standing in the back of the line fell backwards under the power first. Then the next ones fell, until the whole section fell as though a giant vacuum had sucked them down from the back of the line so no one could think they were just a bunch of dominoes that were tumbling against each other. *"The glory of the LORD [had] filled the temple"* (2 Chron. 7:1)!

There was an eighty-four-year-old lady present who was exuberant with holy laughter. She could not get up off the floor. Every time she would try to stand up, she would fall down again. She said to me, "You know, in about 1905 or 1906 when this great revival started, I saw the glory of God. I saw the glory of God in all church services, but I have never seen it from that day to this." She really rolled her eyes as she made that statement. Then she added, "The glory of God has filled this temple tonight."

The pastor of this great church said, "I've been in Pentecost all of my life, and I have never seen anything like I saw happen tonight."

Arise, shine; for thy light is come, and the glory of the LORD is risen upon thee. For, behold, the darkness shall cover the earth, and gross darkness the people: but the LORD shall arise upon thee, and his glory shall be seen upon thee.   (Isa. 60:1–2 KJV)

That means the glory of the Lord is going to be seen on you. These are the days when we are to walk in the glory of God.

Azusa Again?

Why was the glory seen so much at the turn of the last century? I believe it was because those people were hungry, hungry, hungry for the glory of God. When we become that hungry again, we will begin to walk once more where Jesus wants us to walk—in the glory of God!

"But we all, with open face beholding as in a glass the glory of the Lord, are changed into the same image from glory to glory, even as by the Spirit of the Lord" (2 Cor. 3:18 KJV). That's the way we ought to live at all times, *"from glory to glory."* There's no reason for valleys. Let's go from glory to glory.

Moses was out herding sheep when suddenly a bush started burning, but it wasn't consumed. (See Exod. 3:2–5.) He saw the glory of God as God spoke to him, telling him to quit herding sheep and start herding people. That was the beginning of the call of God upon Moses' life—the leading of the children of Israel out of captivity. Actually, Moses depicted a type of Jesus leading people out of sin. The glory of God will still draw people out of their sins.

What is the glory of God? What mystery can it be? How can you know the glory of God? When is it going to come? How is it going to fit into your life? How are you going to fit into the glory of God? Can you see it? Can you hear it? Is it like a *"rushing mighty wind"* (Acts 2:2)? Is it like a burning bush? What is it like? How can you behold it? How can we in the twenty-first century know the glory of God like Moses did?

Saul of Tarsus had persecuted the Christians, even killing many of them. Even though he thought he was a friend of God, Saul was an archenemy of Jesus. When he met Jesus Christ personally, the glory of God shining out from Jesus was so overwhelming that Saul fell backwards under the power of God. (See Acts 9:3–18.) The glory of God was too much for him to behold. He fell backwards! As a result of that, Saul of Tarsus got saved and baptized with the Holy Spirit. He was blinded! He was healed! He spoke in tongues. Then he went out and preached the Gospel and wrote more of the New Testament than anyone else, because the glory of God had touched his life!

Oh, that God would knock a few more Sauls of Tarsus off their high horses and let them see the glory of God so they would sweep across this nation, across the world, changing lives for Jesus because they had seen the glory of God!

This is the day in which God is displaying His glory mightily, so more than ever we need to believe that God is a supernatural God. Jesus is supernatural. Everything about the two of them is supernatural. We need to believe in the supernatural so that we can see the glory of God. I want to see the power and the majesty and the glory of God every day of my life. I want to see the manifestations of God's power. I want to see cripples healed. I want to see children who were born with parts of their little bodies missing totally healed by the power of God. I want to see the glory of God.

What is the glory of God? It can be many things to many different people. To me, the glory of God is the presence of God in everyday living, Jesus walking inside of us, and Jesus doing through us the same things He did when He was on the earth. The Word of God being fulfilled within the life of every believer is the manifested glory of God!

Did it ever dawn on you that Jesus Christ living in your heart is really the glory of God? I want you to walk down the street and just quietly say to yourself, "Jesus is living in here. Jesus is living in here. Jesus is living in here."

Every time you put your foot down, say, "That's the footprint of Jesus. That's the footprint of Jesus. That's the footprint of Jesus."

When you stretch your hand forth to help someone or lay hands on them for healing, say, "These are the hands of Jesus. These are the hands of Jesus. These are the hands of Jesus."

When we begin to speak it aloud and begin to believe it with our minds, our souls, and every beat of our hearts, we will be walking in the glory of God.

I want to see the latter rain. I want to see the former rain. I want to see them both come together, which is what is happening today. God is accelerating His final thrust before Jesus returns. I want to see the glory cloud of God in services when believers gather together and the glory cloud just fills the place with the presence of God.

I want to see angels. I want to see angels ministering and helping people as we go along in our day-by-day work. That's the glory of God.

I want to see hundreds, thousands, millions of people saved. That's the glory of God!

We will never see it if we don't believe. If we will just believe, the glory God will pour out upon us will be amazing.

There's an old song we sang at one of our camp meetings called, "I'm under the Spout Where the Glory Comes Out." That is where I want to sit all the time. That is where I want to be. Do you know why I want to be there? Because that is where Jesus sat.

Jesus sat under the glory spout of God and even though He went to the cross for you and me, He went in the glory of God. Because of the tremendous sacrifice God made and Jesus willingly fulfilled, you and I can walk in the power and the glory and the majesty of God today!

Think Glory! Jesus does.

But seek first the kingdom of God and His righteousness,
and all these things shall be added to you.
—Matthew 6:33

Ten

Nuggets of Truth
Prayer, Forgiveness, Treasures, and Seeking Him First

Almost every verse marked in red in the New Testament (words spoken by Jesus) gives us some special insight into how we should think, but there isn't room in a single book to expand on all of them, so I have selected a few on various subjects that can help make your thinking patterns begin to flow in the same manner as those of Jesus.

Prayer

Jesus spent a lot of time on the earth praying. There were times when He would pray day and night. Therefore, if we have the mind of Christ, we are going to also spend a lot of time in prayer, which in reality is just talking to God and listening to Him.

Charles and I pray constantly, every waking moment. Someone once said to us, "I'm sure you have callouses on your knees from praying." They were surprised by our answer because we very rarely pray on our knees. We pray all the time, and it would be difficult to get our work done if we were on our knees all the time. It would be impossible to write a book on your knees. We need to learn that praying is a twenty-four-hour-a-day activity, or at least every waking moment, and not something that has to be done on your knees.

A Simple Definition

Prayer is communication with God however you do it. All our thoughts are filtered through God, and we talk to Him (think to Him) all day long, in all our business details, in all our planning for meetings, in all our travel arrangements, in all the books we write, and in all the letters we write. Prayer should be such a natural thing that we do it all the time.

There will be special times when you want to do nothing but pray, and draw yourself aside for that purpose, but for the most part, we find the greatest effective prayer life involves an "online" communication with God all the time. We never take our thoughts off God, regardless of what we are doing!

I learned something especially interesting recently concerning the Scripture in Matthew 18:19–20.

Again I tell you, if two of you on earth agree (harmonize together, together make a symphony) about—anything and everything—whatever they shall ask, it will come to pass and be done for them by My Father in heaven. For wherever two or three are gathered (drawn together as My followers) in (into) My name, there I AM in the midst of them. (AMP)

We need to learn to "agree" in prayer. What happens if two people are not completely agreed in prayer? Think about with whom you might be agreeing. Are your beliefs in total agreement, or are you agreeing in certain areas only? We might be in agreement on a certain prayer answer, and yet totally disagree in other scriptural areas. We need to get all of our disagreements ironed out before we begin to agree in prayer. Jesus said where two or three were drawn together as His followers, or believers, He would be right there.

Maybe we won't always get prayers answered because we have failed to realize that in possessing the mind of Christ, we need to know and believe that when we gather two or three people together to pray, we need to gather two or three people who are "all the way" believers of the Lord Jesus. When there is disagreement in any area of God's Word, this means you are not in agreement. Let's choose as prayer partners those with whom our spirits blend and our beliefs blend; then watch for those answers!

You might say, "What if you pray outside the will of God?" Can you really pray outside the will of God if you are totally connected to the Lord Jesus Christ? If Jesus lives in us, and we are operating with His mind at all times, our desires are not going to be outside of what Jesus Himself would pray.

We Will Want What He Wants!

For assuredly, I say to you, whoever says to this mountain, "Be removed and be cast into the sea," and does not doubt in his heart, but believes that those things he says will be done, he will have whatever he says. Therefore I say to you, whatever things you ask when you pray, believe that you receive them, and you will have them. (Mark 11:23–24)

Because Jesus lives in us, and we have the mind of Christ, we are not going to let doubt and unbelief come into our minds. Doubt and unbelief are strictly from the Devil, and since we possess the very mind of Christ, there is no room for Devil thoughts. We're going to pray exactly like Jesus did. We're going to believe exactly the way Jesus did. We're going to expect the same answers to our prayers that Jesus did. We are going to rejoice because we know the answer is on the way.

Forgiveness

Jesus puts a very interesting condition on the end of those Scriptures concerning prayer. He gives the secret as to why many prayers are not answered. Verse 25 says,

> *And whenever you stand praying, if you have anything against anyone, forgive him, that your Father in heaven may also forgive you your trespasses. But if you do not forgive, neither will your Father in heaven forgive your trespasses.*

We are so blessed to have Jesus living in us, and we possess the very mind of Christ. What, then, are we going to do about forgiveness? If you have been wondering why prayers have not been answered, this is the time to search your heart and say, "God, is there any unforgiveness in my heart whatsoever?"

I had been a Christian for many years before I saw the significance of forgiveness. The day God wrote those Scriptures in neon lights before my eyes was the day I really searched my heart to find out if there was any unforgiveness there, and I discovered there was.

A man had stolen $12,000 from our ministry through a dishonest business dealing, and we had some real unforgiveness against him. When we realized this, we forgave him, and within two weeks God sent us a check for $50,000 for the ministry from a totally different source! Forgiveness pays off!

Sometimes we don't activate all of the mind of Christ that is available to us because we don't really understand all of the things God's Word says. Jesus did not go around with unforgiveness in His heart; therefore, we should not feel justified when we say, "Well, look at what he did to me. I have a right not to forgive him." Jesus expects us to forgive anyone whom we have anything against so that there will be no hindrance to our prayers.

I almost explode when I think about such a wonderful, loving Father who says we can have anything we say, providing we have no doubt that we're going to receive it—providing we do not have unforgiveness in our hearts. Because we do have the very mind of Christ, at all times we are going to forgive those who have sinned against us.

Jesus had a wonderful prayer life because He always had an open two-way communication line to God. Because He lives in us and we possess the same mind Jesus has, we, too, can have an open communication to the heavenly Father at all times. God is as close as your spiritual telephone; all you have to do is pick it up, and you'll never get a busy signal with God.

Here's a great verse to remember: *"So shall My word be that goes forth from My mouth; it shall not return to Me void, but it shall accomplish what I please, and it shall prosper in the thing for which I sent it"* (Isa. 55:11).

If we are going to have the same kind of prayer life Jesus had, we are going to have to stand on God's Word and know there is no promise in the Word of God that is ever going to return to us void. We are going to know we can rely on every promise in the Word of God, because not one word of it has ever failed!

When we pray we need to know the things we can receive. When we allow *"this mind"* to be in us, *"which was also in Christ Jesus"* (Phil. 2:5), it will keep us within the Word of God and will give us a desire to pray for the things of God to be completed in our lives, rather than the lust and the pleasures in this world.

We're going to have belief and not doubt in our hearts. Sometimes we look at the circumstances and think there is absolutely no way out. Yet I wonder what we might have done under the same circumstances had we been Jesus when He was nailed to the cross. Would we have thought at that particular time, "God has forgotten all about me?" Would we have looked at the circumstances and said, "This is it; I've had it?" Would we have let fear grip us when we went down into the very depths of hell itself, or would we have known that our prayers to God were answered and that God would protect us in all areas?

Jesus prayed, *"O My Father, if it is possible, let this cup pass from Me; nevertheless, not as I will, but as You will"* (Matt. 26:39). He knew the purpose for which He had been sent to earth. He knew when He went into hell He was going to come right out of there and sit at the right hand of God, the Father Almighty. There was no doubt whatsoever in His mind about His resurrection.

Beloved, let us believe as Jesus did. Let us believe in the promises of God without doubt, without unbelief, without compromise, without wavering. Let us possess and use the mind of Christ where prayer is concerned.

What about Treasures?

Do not lay up for yourselves treasures on earth, where moth and rust destroy and where thieves break in and steal; but lay up for yourselves treasures in heaven, where neither moth nor rust destroys and where thieves do not break in and steal. For where your treasure is, there your heart will be also.
(Matt. 6:19–21)

Because one of our most priceless possessions is the mind of Christ, we have the same attitudes and same thoughts as Jesus Christ. We are not going to be interested in storing up things for ourselves down here.

I once heard a Catholic priest say, "The only thing a dead man holds in his hands are the things he has given to God." How true. When they put your body in a casket, they can put a fur coat on you, they can wrap you in your finest mink, they can load your hands with diamonds, but it won't do the least bit of good. All we are going to take out of this earth are the things we've given to God. We ought to be extremely interested in our heavenly bank accounts.

One of the best deposits we can ever make into our heavenly bank account is a deposit slip showing the names of the souls of people who might not have ever met Jesus if we had not shared the Gospel with them. We can give glory to God, which is one of the greatest ways I know of to store up treasures in heaven. We can lay hands on the sick and heal them, and we know this gives God tremendous joy. Put those things in your bank account that add up in heaven instead of earthly bank accounts that mean nothing to God!

Allowing the mind of Christ to be in you means that you are not going to be laying up the glory of this world.

We are not going to be laying up the deceit of this world.

We are not going to be storing up the kind of riches down here that people think are so important. Sometimes we think this means only money, but there are many other things people feel bring glory.

How many times have we seen TV and Hollywood stars rise up rapidly to fame and fortune? All their earthly treasures are invested in the flimsy values and glory that temporarily accompany them. When their world crashes, they and their earthly treasures often end in suicide.

The Word says, *"Lay up for yourselves treasures in heaven"* (Matt. 6:20). What are our treasures? They are the very desires of our hearts—the very things we hold near and dear to us.

Let the things that you hold dear be exactly the things Jesus valued. What did He value? He valued the souls of humans, the health and healing of humans, and the deliverance of humans. He held God dear to His heart.

If we are to store up treasures in heaven where nothing can ever get in and disturb or destroy them, we must learn to develop the attributes of Jesus. We can then store the things that are pleasing to God in our heavenly bank account, the things that are the very mind of Christ.

Matthew 11:28–30 gives us some wonderful words from Jesus:

Come to Me, all you who labor and are heavy laden, and I will give you rest. Take My yoke upon you and learn from Me, for I am gentle and lowly in heart, and you will find rest for your souls. For My yoke is easy and My burden is light.

I'm going to believe with all my heart, my mind, my body, and my soul that the yoke Jesus gives us is not a heavy yoke. His burden is light. We do not have to be burdened down with the cares of the world. We do not have to be worried all the time because He says, "You take My yoke because My burden is light, and I'll take care of your life for you."

I especially love the *Amplified* version. It reads, *"I will ease and relieve and refresh your souls....My yoke is wholesome, (useful, good)—not harsh, hard, sharp or pressing, but comfortable, gracious and pleasant; and My burden is light and easy to be borne"* (Matt. 11:28, 30). Glory! Give all your burdens to Him!

We know all these wonderful promises of God, but we need to have them brought to the surface occasionally in a different way, or at a different time. An "oldie" that is a favorite of mine is,

> *The Kingdom of Heaven is like a treasure a man discovered in a field. In his excitement, he sold everything he owned to get enough money to buy the field—and get the treasure, too! Again, the Kingdom of Heaven is like a pearl merchant on the lookout for choice pearls. He discovered a real bargain—a pearl of great value—and sold everything he owned to purchase it!* (Matt. 13:44–46 TLB)

Possessing the mind of Christ, we should see exactly what Jesus was saying. Very simply He was saying, "If you will give up everything and follow Me, then that is worth more than anything in the whole world. It's worth everything to follow Me!" One man sold *everything* to receive the treasure in the field, and one man sold *everything* to get the pearl of great price.

An Invisible Pearl

The pearl of great price in all of our lives is not something we can wear around our neck, nor a pearl we can put in a ring on our finger. It is a pearl we keep in our hearts, that personal relationship with the Lord Jesus Christ. Nothing on this earth can compare with the privilege of having a personal relationship with the Lord Jesus Christ. There are no treasures on this earth; there is no money on this earth; there are no riches on this earth that will compare with the knowledge that we personally have Jesus Christ in our hearts!

We need to "sell" ourselves for the pearl of great price!

Another of my favorite portions of Scripture that I practice is found in Matthew 6:25–34:

> *So my counsel is: Don't worry about things—food, drink, and clothes. For you already have life and a body—and they are far more important than what to eat and wear. Look at the birds! They don't worry about what to eat—they don't need to sow or reap or store up food—for your heavenly Father feeds them. And you are far more valuable to him than they are. Will all your worries add a single moment to your life? And why worry about your clothes? Look at the field lilies! They don't worry about theirs. Yet King Solomon in all his glory was not clothed as beautifully as they. And if God cares so wonderfully for flowers that are here today and gone tomorrow, won't he more surely care for you, O men of little faith? So don't worry at all about having enough food and clothing.*

Why be like the heathen? For they take pride in all these things and are deeply concerned about them. But your heavenly Father already knows perfectly well that you need them, and he will give them to you if you give him first place in your life and live as he wants you to. So don't be anxious about tomorrow. God will take care of your tomorrow too. Live one day at a time. (TLB)

We worry and worry and worry about how we are going to be fed. What is going to happen during the famine that is coming? What is going to happen because of inflation? What is going to happen due to recession? Why worry? The Bible specifically tells us not to be like the heathen who worry, but to be like the field lilies.

Philippians 4:19 says, *"But my God shall supply all your need according to his riches in glory by Christ Jesus"* (KJV).

He will, without a shadow of a doubt, take care of me and my family as long as we are in His will. I know that I know that I know this to be a fact. God says it, so I believe it! He also says to work hard and to use common sense. He doesn't agree to do *my* part in my earthly responsibilities. I have to do my part. He will then do His part.

As we think the thoughts of Jesus, we know that God will provide for our every need. Therefore, I am not going to worry about the things of today. I am not going to worry about the problems that might come up tomorrow, because I know that God is going to take care of them.

What do we do instead of worrying? We take Matthew 6:33 and pretend that it is a press-on decal; I iron it right onto my heart. *"But seek first the kingdom of God and His righteousness, and all these things shall be added to you."* The Living Bible so beautifully and simply expresses it by saying, *"He will give them to you if you give him first place in your life and live as he wants you to."*

The best insurance you can have in the entire world is simply a decision to give God first place in your life. Then you will have that beautiful peace that says that God will take care of every need you have.

Seek first of all the very righteousness of God! Seek to possess the mind of Christ at all times. Seek to use the mind of Christ at all times. Seek to think with the mind of Christ at all times. Then, and only then, will you find that all of these things will be added unto you.

Kingdom-Seeking Produced My Heart's Desire

One of the greatest examples of that verse in my personal life concerned marriage. When I met Charles, I could not see how I could possibly get married. God had placed such a call upon my life that I knew I had no choice except to serve Him.

Being a housewife just didn't fit into the schedule God had given me. Yet God had suddenly put a charming man in my path. My heart was beating for Charles. My very soul was crying out for Charles. Yet because of the call God had put on my life, I could not see any possible way to get married and fit a husband into my life.

One Sunday afternoon, in a spare bedroom of a pastor's home in Florida, God spoke to me very distinctly. "You are to marry Charles," He said. "Because you have sought first My kingdom and My righteousness, I am going to add a husband to your life—a husband to protect you, a husband to take care of you, a husband to love you all of the days of your life."

Had I sought Charles as a husband, I probably would not be Mrs. Charles Hunter today.

Because I sought first the kingdom of God and His righteousness, because possessing the mind of Christ kept my mind on the things of God instead of on the things that I might naturally want as a woman, God rewarded my obedience. He brought me the desire of my heart—the most wonderful, loving husband in the whole world.

We need to develop our minds to the point where we will have such a craving and such a hunger for the Word of God that nothing else will satisfy us. Truthfully, nothing else can satisfy us. Because of this hunger, we will continue to seek, to search, to look for, to pursue, and to hunt for nothing but the kingdom of God! Then we will be so blessed to discover how all of these other things will, little by little and one by one, be added unto us.

Letting this mind be in you that was also in Christ Jesus is the most beautiful, simple, easy way in the world to receive all of the desires of your heart!

Take delight in the Lord, and He will give you the desires. Then, when He puts His desires into our hearts, He will give us the desires of our hearts because they are His desires for us.

The Spirit of the LORD is upon Me, because He has anointed
Me to preach the gospel to the poor.
—Luke 4:18

Eleven

The Anointing

---•---

The Spirit of the Lord GOD is upon Me, because the LORD has anointed Me to preach good tidings to the poor; He has sent Me to heal the brokenhearted, to proclaim liberty to the captives, and the opening of the prison to those who are bound; to proclaim the acceptable year of the LORD, and the day of vengeance of our God; to comfort all who mourn, to console those who mourn in Zion, to give them beauty for ashes, the oil of joy for mourning, the garment of praise for the spirit of heaviness; that they may be called trees of righteousness, the planting of the LORD, that He may be glorified. —Isaiah 61:1–3

There are many different opinions today of what the anointing really is and how many different kinds of anointings there are.

One of the most important things to remember is that when you are born again, Jesus Christ lives on the inside of you. One of the most critical things we can ever learn in all of our Christian lives is to know that we know that we know that Jesus has taken up residence inside us! Paul preached over and over again, *"Christ in you, the hope of glory"* (Col. 1:27).

Christianity is not a religion—it is a way of life! It is a 24-hours-a-day walking with the knowledge that Jesus Christ lives inside you. It is knowing that you are doing the things that Jesus did because of the awesome fact that He lives inside you!

If Jesus lives inside you and He is anointed, then what are you? Obviously, you are anointed. If He is in you, His anointing is going to be in you and flow out of you! He gives an eternal, everlasting anointing, not an anointing that comes and goes.

The anointing was not given to Jesus just for Him to hold it in His hand and say, "Look what I have. I have a special anointing. I have been anointed" and then do nothing with it. You have been anointed for exactly the same purpose Jesus was—to do things! The anointing is not given to you as something for you to admire or to brag about. The anointing is something for you to do something with! Jesus said, *"He has anointed Me to preach the gospel to the poor"* (Luke 4:18). That is a responsibility you and I have. If we are anointed with Jesus living inside us, and we are, then we are to preach the Gospel to the poor. In other words, we are to share Jesus with every person we meet!

Restoration for All

Jesus went on to say, *"He has sent Me to heal the brokenhearted"* (v. 18). One of the things we need to do is to reach out in love to those people who are brokenhearted for whatever reason.

We are to *"preach deliverance to the captives"* (v. 18 KJV). There are multitudes of people who are in bondage to many different things. We can be in bondage to a spirit of religion instead of walking in the freedom of a personal relationship with the Lord Jesus Christ.

"And the opening of the prison to those who are bound" (Isa. 61:1). There are many people who are behind prison bars who have more freedom than some of us who live on the outside simply because we are bound by a spirit of religion. We are bound by tradition, which does not allow us to enjoy Jesus Christ the way we should.

We can be in bondage to bad attitudes. We can be in bondage to poverty. We can be in bondage to money. We can be in bondage to habits such as cigarettes, alcohol, and drugs. We need to proclaim liberty to those who are being held captive by any one of these things!

We are *"to proclaim the acceptable year of the LORD"* (v. 2). It is our responsibility and privilege at all times to tell everybody that Jesus saves and that Jesus wants everybody to be saved!

We are *"to comfort all who mourn, to console those who mourn in Zion, to give them beauty for ashes, the oil of joy for mourning"* (vv. 2–3).

In the case of the departure of a loved one, there is a time when we need to mourn, but there is also a time when we need to get over it. We need to give the grieving the oil of joy because when you have Jesus, He is your joy, hope, peace, and assurance.

Look forward to "what you can do for Him, not what He can do for you." When we are busy doing what Jesus told us to do (Mark 16:15–18), we quit looking inward and feeling sorry for ourselves. When we are bringing the life of Jesus for all eternity to others, the light of God will shine brightly through us! The more we lift up Jesus, the bigger He will become and the smaller our problems become. Talking about our problems will make them bigger and Jesus smaller! The Bible tells us that *"no one, having put his hand to the plow, and looking back, is fit for the kingdom of God"* (Luke 9:62). Because of this, we cannot look backward. We must look forward and go on with our lives.

We are directed to give people *"the garment of praise for the spirit of heaviness; that they may be called the trees of righteousness, the planting of the Lord, that He may be glorified"* (Isa. 61:3).

Did you ever wake up on a Sunday morning and feel like you didn't want to go to church because your arthritis was hurting or you just didn't feel good? That's the very time we need to get up and to force ourselves to go to church. Once you walk in, even carrying a spirit of heaviness, and get involved in the praise and worship and actually put on the garment of praise, you will discover that the spirit of heaviness leaves!

It is so important that we have the joy of the Lord in our hearts at all times because the Bible says that we are the trees of righteousness, the planting of the Lord. Many times the only Jesus anyone will ever see is the Jesus they see in you and in me.

In Luke 4:18–19 we see the same words repeated. In Isaiah this is a prophetic utterance concerning Jesus. In the fourth chapter of Luke once again the same words are repeated. They are extremely important to understanding the anointing.

Luke 4:16–21 reads,

So He came to Nazareth, where He had been brought up. And as His custom was, He went into the synagogue on the Sabbath day, and stood up to read. And He was handed the book of the prophet Isaiah. And when He had opened the book, He found the place where it was written: "The Spirit of the LORD is upon Me, because He has anointed Me to preach the gospel to the poor; He has sent Me to heal the brokenhearted, to proclaim liberty to the captives and recovery of sight to the blind, to set at liberty those who are oppressed; to proclaim the acceptable year of the LORD." Then He closed the book, and gave it back to the attendant and sat down. And the eyes of all who were in the synagogue were fixed on Him. And He began to say to them, "Today this Scripture is fulfilled in your hearing."

This passage of Scripture is vitally important in order for us to understand what the anointing is and why we possess it.

These are basically the same words that were spoken in Isaiah. However, in Isaiah it was a prophetic utterance and in the book of Luke it is Jesus "in the now."

Verse 20 says,

Then He closed the book, and gave it back to the attendant and sat down. And the eyes of all who were in the synagogue were fixed on Him. And He began to say to them, "Today this Scripture is fulfilled in your hearing."

When Jesus said, *"Today this Scripture is fulfilled in your hearing,"* it broke a mental block for a lot of people! Jesus and the Word are one, so Jesus stepped out of the Book at that particular time in history, *"and the Word became flesh and dwelt among us"* (John 1:14).

No longer could Jesus be contained behind the walls of a church or behind stained glass windows because the Word had become flesh. He stepped totally and completely out of the Book, and then the miracles began to happen. Once again, He emphasized the fact that He had been anointed, but receiving an anointing is for the purpose of preaching the Gospel to the poor, of healing the brokenhearted, preaching deliverance to the captives, recovery of sight to blind, setting at liberty those who are oppressed, and preaching the acceptable year of the Lord!

When we look over the things He said, we know that we are anointed because He is living in us, and He is anointed!

I believe with all my heart that the Spirit of the Lord is upon me. There is no doubt in my mind whatsoever. Why? Because Jesus lives in me. Therefore I am going to do exactly as He did, and I am going to say exactly the same things He said.

When you say and believe that the Spirit of the Lord is upon you, it will give you your spiritual goose pimples for the day!

The Spirit of the Lord is upon you.

The spirit of the Devil isn't upon you.

The Spirit of the Lord is upon you. That is an overwhelming, awesome statement! It is a difficult thing to understand, but we need to believe it.

You have been anointed! Therefore, the same abilities that rested on Jesus, the same privileges, the same responsibilities, the same power that rested on Him, rest on you.

We don't have to go around pleading and begging and crying, "Oh, God, anoint me. Oh, God, anoint me. Oh, God, anoint me. Oh, God, anoint me." You have been anointed, and therefore, you are anointed.

You need to believe that you have been anointed by God and act on it!

Jesus didn't say, "You have been anointed, and that anointing stays there for thirty minutes." He said, "You have been anointed permanently." We read in 1 John 2:27, *"But the anointing which you have received from Him abides in you."* The word *abide* means to "continue permanently!" You can stop right here and say out loud, "I have been anointed!"

We believe an anointing will be on those born-again believers who have made a total, absolute commitment of their lives to God and who have died to self. The baptism with fire comes with the death of the old self-nature; then nothing is left of self except dead ashes. That's what happened to sin offerings in the Old Testament. They were burned until only dead ashes were left. When you die totally to self and all you want to do is to pour your whole self into ministering to others, the anointing will always be there.

It is always the anointing that breaks the yoke.

On the first night of all crusades, Charles talks to the ushers, and I take charge of setting up the books. Recently, a lady came by and said, "Are you touching those books?"

"Yes, I'm touching the books."

She said, "Aren't you afraid you'll lose the anointing?"

I said, "No, do you know why? I have been anointed to preach the Gospel, and it is not going to fall off me because I touch a book!" His anointing is not fragile.

A man asked, "Do you dare talk to people before a service?"

"Yes, I dare talk to people before a service."

"Well, don't you lose the anointing?"

"No, I won't lose the anointing because I have been anointed *permanently* to preach the Gospel." The anointing doesn't come and go like the waves of the ocean. You have either been anointed or you haven't been anointed. Either Jesus lives in you or He doesn't!

Why is the anointing permanent? First John 2:28 says, *"And now, little children, abide* [live, remain permanently] *in Him."*

I wasn't anointed before I got saved. But I have been anointed now because I am a child of God. I possess the mind of Christ. I am born again, and Jesus lives in me; therefore, I have been anointed, and the anointing is there at all times.

I like to mingle with people before a meeting. I like to autograph books. I love to talk to people. I love to touch them. I love to have them touch me. I love to get hugged, and I love to hug them back.

At a convention in Atlanta, Georgia, the doors to the meeting room hadn't opened. There was a lady in a wheelchair in the hall. I didn't wait until I got into the meeting to minister to her. I didn't have to "work up" an anointing, and I wasn't afraid that I didn't have an anointing. I believe the anointing is there at all times to speak a word that needs to be spoken, to lay hands upon the sick and to heal them.

I said, "Wouldn't you rather walk into this meeting than be wheeled in?"

She said, "Yes."

I laid hands on her and said, "In Jesus' name," and out of that wheelchair she came!

Do I lose the anointing when I mingle with people and talk with them before the service? Does it fly out the window if someone gets healed before the service? No, your anointing is with you at all times. All you have to do is believe it and use it!

If you have the anointing of God only upon special occasions, then you will never be able to minister to the world out there when you go into the grocery store, restaurant, dry cleaner's, or other stores to shop. You are anointed at all times if you really believe it, and whatever comes out of your mouth is anointed of God.

The words we speak are Spirit and they are life!

"A good man out of the good treasure of his heart brings forth good; and an evil man out of the evil treasure of his heart brings forth evil. For out of the abundance of the heart his mouth speaks" (Luke 6:45).

Because Jesus lives in me, I have to believe that what comes out of my mouth is going to be pure and good if my heart is good and my heart is pure. I have to believe what Jesus said because my mind operates in exactly the same channel His does. Jesus makes it so plain to me that when my heart is right, out of my mouth will come good things— things that will bless people, things that will thrill people, things that will inspire people, and not things that will tear people down.

What is stored up in the heart of an upright, honorable, or intrinsically good man will produce that same kind of good.

If I speak evil out of my mouth, it is because there is evil in my heart. If an evil man stores up in his storehouse those things that are depraved, that is exactly what is going to come out of his mouth. Praise God, we can bring forth out of our mouths those things that are pleasing, acceptable, and delightful to God by storing them in our hearts.

As we continued talking about our video schools and how God can supernaturally do things through video schools, a man came over to us. Now watch what your anointed words, spoken in a public restaurant, can do.

He said, "I heard you talking about my Father."

I said, "Really?"

"Yes!"

We said, "You must be talking about God."

He said, "I am. I was fascinated as I sat there and listened to every word you said, because you didn't talk about anything else."

He asked us where we went to church. We asked, "Where do you go to church?"

He said, "I just moved to town, and I was looking for a church where the people talk about Jesus!"

Would you believe anointed words could go out over a bowl of spinach? They really did because that man heard them. And so we had an opportunity to witness to him about freedom in Jesus and about what was happening at the Hunter Ministries.

I think it's exciting when you sit at a table in a restaurant and realize people can hear everything you are saying and to know that your words are anointed. Next time you go into a restaurant or a cafeteria, just look around and think, "My words are anointed. They're hitting that table. They're hitting that table. They're hitting that table." Just imagine yourself with little anointed sparks flying out of your mouth and hitting the people at tables all around you.

You never really know what can happen when you begin to believe that your words are powerfully anointed. "Wow! Jesus lives in me! I have a special anointing because I have the same anointing Jesus had, and so when I speak the Word, whether it's over spinach or cauliflower, roast beef or fish, Mexican food or Chinese food, those are anointed words that can go out and touch somebody."

Electronically Transmitted Anointing

I believe that I'm anointed. I believe that when I speak into a television camera, the anointing of God goes right into it. I believe there are going to be people who will watch some of our miracle services on video and when Charles and I raise our hands to heal the sick, people watching the video on television sets are going to fall out under the power of God. I believe it!

Do you know what else I believe? I believe the same thing is going to happen to you if you can just get the simplicity of this truth into your mind: "I have been anointed. I have been anointed. I have been anointed." The day that you don't feel very anointed is the day you need to say a hundred times, "I'm anointed. I'm anointed. I'm anointed. I'm anointed. I don't feel like it but I'm anointed. I'm anointed. I'm anointed. It doesn't slide off me when I don't feel good."

The anointing of God is present at all times.

It is a tremendous thing to know that you are anointed. There are times when I have gotten into the car, possibly to go to a local engagement, after I've been involved in work at the office. Proofreading to make sure there are no misspelled words in a new book or a magazine article is not really very spiritual because that is routine, nitty-gritty work.

The first thing I always say when I rush out of the office is, "God, I thank You that even though I don't feel anointed, I am anointed because You said in Your Word that I have been anointed."

"To set at liberty them that are bruised" (Luke 4:18 KJV). There are many people in the world today who are bruised. It's our responsibility to know we're so anointed that our anointed words can go out and heal those who have been bruised by life.

People are bruised by what the world has done to them; bruised by what some friend has said to them; bruised by a set of circumstances that in the natural looks impossible, but in the supernatural is absolutely fantastic!

Now, that didn't say "to heal the sick"; it said, *"to heal the brokenhearted"* (v. 18). Do you really believe the Word of God coming out of your lips can heal the brokenhearted?

When I was young, every girl had a broken heart every weekend because boyfriends changed girlfriends and went out with somebody else. "Oh, I'm crushed! I'll never fall in love again." Did you ever say that? And then you went right out and fell in love all over again until the next weekend!

That's not the kind of a broken heart I mean. There are people whose lives have gotten into such a mess that there is no way in the natural that they can get out of it. We have been sent to heal those brokenhearted people.

Healing the brokenhearted does not mean sympathizing with them. Sympathy points to self, causing people to look inward, which is a tool of the Devil. Sympathy will only intensify their grief and sorrow. We have been sent to mend, to cure, to repair, to restore, and to ease the pain of the one who is brokenhearted.

We are to preach *"deliverance to the captives"* (v. 18 KJV). Who needs deliverance? Anyone who is in bondage needs deliverance. If people are in bondage to alcohol, they need to be delivered from alcohol! Many times when we think about preaching deliverance to the poor, we think about demon-possessed people. There are many people who are bound by alcohol, drugs, dope, cigarettes, illicit sex, depression, guilt, hate, and other types of sin. They are bound by an evil force. We need to minister deliverance to them. We need to set them free in the name of Jesus!

People can be in chains of fear. They can be in the most horrible bondage in the world to money. They can be in bondage to money whether they are rich or poor. Poor people are in bondage because they don't have enough money to pay their bills. Sometimes rich people are in bondage to money because money is their god. We often think we are to preach deliverance only to the poor in finances. Sometimes the poor are the richest, and the richest are the poorest.

We are to preach deliverance to the financially poor person, too. To tell him we have been set free from the curse of the law, which is sin, death, sickness, and poverty. We have been set free! And we can tell that person, "You can be set free from sin, sickness, and poverty right now!"

We are to tell the homosexual there is deliverance! Then we must minister deliverance!

We are to tell the sick there is healing in the name of Jesus! Then minister healing!

We are to cast out devils and set the oppressed free!

You might shudder at the idea of casting out devils until you fully realize that your mind is on the same wavelength as Jesus. Then you won't shy away. You will look at them with eyes of compassion and anger—compassion for the ones who are possessed and anger at the Devil who has attacked them!

When you realize the responsibility you have because you possess the mind of Christ, you will cast out devils and set people free!

"To preach the acceptable year of the Lord" (Luke 4:19 KJV). You have been anointed to preach the acceptable year of the Lord! What is the acceptable year of the Lord? Right now. Every year is the acceptable year of the Lord! Today *"is the day of salvation"* (2 Cor. 6:2)!

"I'm anointed!"

Say it at the top of your lungs! "I'M ANOINTED!"

Then I said, "Here am I! Send me."
—Isaiah 6:8

Twelve

The Great Commission

———————●———————

Jesus really poured out His compassionate heart when He gave the Great Commission. He imparted some real specifics, simply presented, so that the world could understand what He was saying.

Please do not ignore His last instructions to us!

None of us has any problem understanding what He said about preaching the Gospel. Yet we pay very little attention to it. *"And He said to them, 'Go into all the world and preach the gospel to every creature. He who believes and is baptized will be saved; but he who does not believe will be condemned'"* (Mark 16:15–16). Not a single believer could ever misconstrue what Jesus said, and we have only two choices: obey Him or disobey Him! We have grown so fat spiritually in the last few years that we have ignored His heart-cry to go out and talk to every person we meet so that they can know Him as their Savior. We like to send missionaries overseas, but we need to let the heart of Jesus be so "in us" that our own hearts cry with compassion for the lost.

And these signs will follow those who believe: In My name they will cast out demons; they will speak with new tongues; they will take up serpents; and if they drink anything deadly, it will by no means hurt them; they will lay hands on the sick, and they will recover. *(Mark 16:17–18)*

In this instance, Jesus' heart is not crying out to the sinner, but to the believers—not only to the pastors and evangelists, but to the ordinary, everyday believer. He is telling us that signs and wonders will follow us in our daily walk. He is telling us that we will cast out demons. He is telling us that we will lay hands on the sick, and they will recover! If the Bible is true, then let's get on with it and begin to believe that we can do it, too—not because we make a decision that we can, but because Jesus said it. The only decision we need to make is that we will do it.

When you sincerely understand the message that the Great Commission is for all believers, and not just for a few selected "pets" of God who have special abilities, it will change your entire life. That portion of Scripture is for each and every one of us, because God doesn't have any "pets." (See Acts 10:34.)

God has been stressing in our hearts that most of the body of Christ must begin to obey the command of Jesus in the Great Commission.

He told all of us to go out into the highways and byways to tell others about Him and to give them the Good News in such a way that they will know Him as their Savior and Lord. Some have learned to minister healing to a few, but every believer needs to daily lead people to Jesus with signs and wonders following. Jesus used signs, wonders, and miracles to convince people that He was the Son of God, *"the way, the truth, and the life"* (John 14:6). We must do exactly that in order to totally fulfill the Great Commission.

What will happen when we, the body of Christ, receive the heart and compassion of Jesus to win the lost before it is too late? WOW! It's exciting to even think of the potential!

Let us give a testimony of what has happened in one man's life through the book *How to Heal the Sick.*

A world-known teacher–minister who had, along with his associates and team, for years been teaching laymen of foreign countries how to be pastors received some of our books.

He had never really believed in healing, but through a flier he received in the mail, he ordered our "Supernatural Special," which included *How to Heal the Sick, Supernatural Horizons,* and *Angels on Assignment.* He thought, "I wonder if there is anything to this supernatural thing."

He was leaving the next day for Ghana and took the healing book with him to read on the plane. He had prepared three months for his teaching while in Ghana with two associates.

When he arrived in Ghana, he could not leave for two days because of a shortage of fuel for the jeep, so the three men were stuck in the hotel for two full days and nights.

He was so excited about what he had read in *How to Heal the Sick* that for the two days, the three men took two-hour turns reading the book aloud, absolutely astonished and astounded at what they were learning. They tested it with the Bible, and it was all in line with the Word. It reached their spirits, and God said, "Throw away your other teachings, and teach these people how to heal the sick."

They taught the first day, and that night over 250 ⟨
500 pastors were healed. It actually worked for them, anu
a phenomenal ministry followed. It changed this minister's
life!

How we praise God for what can happen when only one
person gets the message that *"signs* [and wonders] *will follow
those who believe"* (Mark 16:17), and the message that each one
of us is to do the works of Jesus.

God is so strongly impressing us to urgently preach to
everyone we can that each member of the body of Christ must
actually be exactly like Jesus and do all the things He did
while He was the only body of Christ on earth.

Our Holy Challenge

We challenge every pastor to teach everyone in his church
how to heal the sick and how to minister salvation and healing, and then send them out two by two into the homes of
their city and reach everyone in that city for Jesus. It can be
done only with signs and wonders following, but when each
one believes the simple teachings of Jesus, it will work for you
and your people!

This is the last generation to live before the return of
Jesus, and we must win the lost to Jesus quickly! Time is rapidly running out, and the only ones Jesus has to do His work
are those of us who believe.

God has prepared the hearts of the sinners so much that
we hardly need to mention the name of Jesus before they are
ready to accept Him. They have tried everything else, includ-
ing religion, and found that nothing has given them the peace
for which they were searching. God is getting His children

prepared to go tell the sinners what a great thing He has in store for those who will believe in Jesus! We are the only ones He has to do this job, and if we don't do it, people will go into hell forever.

We believe Jesus will baptize you with fire as well as the Holy Spirit, just as He did to the 120 on the Day of Pentecost. He will put a zeal and boldness into you to do mighty works for Him! That is His calling for each of us. Charles and I cannot stop because we have such a burning in our very souls for the lost.

At the meeting where the blue flame appeared, God told us to tell the people that if they would not go out and do His work as Jesus had commanded, He would walk over the heads of the Spirit-filled Christians. He said He would instead save the drug addicts and the outcast and put His Spirit, zeal, and compassion in them, and send them out to do His work because He was going to get His work accomplished!

Charles just made an interesting statement to me as I was finishing the "Glory of God" chapter. He said, "Honey, the glory of God that I really want to see is the hundreds, the thousands, maybe even the millions of people we have touched through our crusades, through television, and through our books, begin to do exactly the same things we are doing and operate in the glory of God; go out and lay hands on the sick and bring people into the kingdom of God."

When you come right down to it, what is the greatest thing in the world you could see? Hundreds of thousands and even millions of people coming to Jesus as a result of something you did.

When we possess the mind of Christ, we want to fulfill the wishes of Jesus. We want to do everything He wants us to do. We want to see the world saved, we want to see the world reclaimed, and we want to see the world led into the kingdom of God!

It's not God's wish that any should perish.

It's not the wish of Jesus that any should perish.

It is Their wish that all should be saved!

Say with Isaiah and with us, "Here am I, Lord, send me!" (See Isaiah 6:8.)

Look among the nations and watch; be utterly astounded!
For I will work a work in your days which you would
not believe, though it were told you.
—Habakkuk 1:5

Thirteen

God's Acceleration

We are living in the most spectacular, fast-moving days of Christian existence! We see a great increase in the tempo of everything God is doing, and as we search the Scriptures, we find that His Word backs up the accelerated speed!

"'Behold, the days are coming,' says the LORD, 'when the plowman shall overtake the reaper, and the treader of grapes him who sows seed'" (Amos 9:13).

Visualize a grape seed being dropped to the ground and springing up before it ever reaches the ground! Branches will come out, leaves will appear, and grapes will suddenly appear on the vine and will ripen. The grapes will be put in the winepress and be treaded on before the seed ever touches the ground! That's fast! That's real acceleration!

This is the awesome type of day in which we are living!

"Look among the nations and watch; be utterly astounded! For I will work a work in your days which you would not believe, though it were told you" (Hab. 1:5).

This is exactly what is happening today! God is doing something so supernatural that it is difficult to believe it even in your wildest imagination.

God spoke six words to Charles on March 31, 1990, "Take a census of the world." These six words impacted our lives forever!

Two months later God spoke again and told us the first census would be taken in Honduras. We trained pastors and leaders, who in turn trained their people. Then we sent them out to knock on every door. During the first two weeks' work, more than 1 million people came into the kingdom of God as a result of the "knocking-on-every-door census." The Gulf War slowed down the census slightly because no gas was available in Honduras, so we left our representative there for a year. By the end of that first year, there were over 2 million people who had documented their salvation in a nation of 5 million people! This is incredible—40 percent of the entire population of a nation accepted Jesus in only one year!

Several years after that, the coordinator for Honduras reported,

> We have seen a tremendous growth in churches. Today, there is fire and excitement for growing! One pastor had about 300 members last year. Now they are reaching 4,000 people. They previously had 50 churches in the country, and now they have 86!
>
> A church in San Pedro Sula had 200 members last year. Now they are reaching 15,000! Another church had about 1,000 members. Now they have around 12,000! Another church had around 700 members. Now they are running multiple services with a total of 6,000 people.

Many, many churches are now regularly running from 1,000 to 5,000 people in their services.

The influence of the Christian church is such a good thing that the president began calling on pastors to pray for the new members of the Supreme Court! Formerly when a problem arose, the union leaders and bank presidents were called, but not anymore. They call the Pentecostal pastors for godly wisdom!

Drugs have gone down, alcohol problems have gone down, the divorce rate has shrunk, the crime problem has shrunk, and the government gives the credit to the census that was taken!

God spoke to us in September of 1996 and said, "Now is the time to go for the entire world." Our spirits were really stirred to action! We called three men whom we knew were qualified and put them on the payroll and said, "Now is the time to start."

Even though our men went to work immediately and were working diligently every day, it seemed that we could not get any nation off dead center to really start the census of knocking on every door in their nation.

Finally the first results came in! The fax machine rang; a fax came through from India in November of 1997 and showed 858,000 documented salvations! We were so excited we didn't know what to do, and then we got the shock of our lives because this news was immediately followed the next day with another 255,000 salvations, making a total of 1,113,000 salvations in two days. This almost completely blew our minds because, not having received anything for such a long time, it came as a total shock with figures our finite minds could hardly accept! When we discovered those salvations came in from an area made up of eighty percent

Muslims and Hindus, the awesomeness of what God was doing was overwhelming!

The incredible thing is, just a day later, we got a report of 273,004 salvations from the Philippines. This was followed on the first of December by another report of 862,661, making a total from the Philippines of 1,135,665! In just one week we had gone from zero to 2,248,665!

Our minds were utterly astounded exactly the way God's Word says because the figures were too large for us to even imagine!

The Holy Spirit told us to send a representative over there to check out the situation because we wanted to make sure that the figures were accurate. The first fax he sent back said, "It is even better than you think!"

The coordinator in the Philippines made an interesting comment to our director. After he had taken him to the first area to show him how he took the census, he made a very wonderful statement: "See how easy it is to win a million people to Jesus!"

When the Holy Spirit leads, it is easy!

You might wonder how this is happening. Within eight months of the first report from India, over 50 million documented salvations from nations all around the world have been reported. All the credit goes to God! In order for this to be accomplished, the method has to be simple, not cluttered and complicated.

Brought by an Angel

It started in a restaurant in Farmington, Missouri, when a man came and sat down at the end of the table and spoke directly to me. He said, "Frances, I know what a fanatic you have always been about winning people to Jesus. I have a new way to show you."

We're always interested in learning new ways to win people to Jesus because that's the burning desire of our hearts at all times. He said, "As soon as the waitress gets to the table I will say to her, 'Did you know there are two kinds of beautiful waitresses in this restaurant?'

"She will say, 'Really?'

"I will say, 'Yes, those who are saved and those who are about to be; which are you?'"

When he said that, something exploded inside me. I felt like a bomb had gone off!

I instantly recognized it was a "win/win" situation, and there was no way you could lose! They are either saved or the only other answer they can give you is, "I am about to be."

I am always eager to try new ways, so I said, "Let me do it. Let me do it. Let me do it. Don't you do it; let *me*." He agreed, so when the waitress came up, I asked her the question that has now become so familiar with us at all times, "Did you know there are two kinds of beautiful waitresses who work in this restaurant?" She said, "Really?" Just like the man said.

I said, "Those who are saved and those who are about to be; which are you?"

I did not expect the type of reply we got at all, so it was a total and complete shock! She simply started crying and said, "I guess I'm the last one." God's Holy Spirit beat me to her, and He had her completely prepared and hungry! I was holding her hand and didn't let it go, so I said, "Wonderful! Repeat this after me: 'Father, forgive my sins. Jesus, come into my heart and make me the kind of person You want me to be. Thank You for saving me.'" She repeated the prayer and once again burst into tears.

I asked her, "Where is Jesus right now?" She looked totally shocked and said, "In my heart!" She was so affected by her salvation that she had to go into the kitchen for about ten minutes and cry before she could come back and wait on us again! It was really a glorious experience, and it taught us something: it is so easy to win people to Jesus in this very simple way.

As soon as I led the waitress to Jesus, the man said, "I wish I could stay for lunch, but I have another appointment," and he got up and left. As soon as he left, I turned to the pastor who was sitting across from me and said, "Who was that man?"

The pastor said, "What man?"

I said, "The man I was talking to who was sitting at the end of the table."

He said, "I didn't see anybody there."

I said, "The man who told me, "There are two kinds of...."

He said, "I thought that was your idea. I didn't hear anybody talking to you."

I thought that was very unusual, but I said, "No, that wasn't my idea at all. That man told me how to do that."

Then I turned to the eight or nine other people who were at the table and asked them if they knew who he was, and two people saw him, but nobody heard him talking except me. I thought this was a little odd, but I just put it aside because at that point I was so excited about looking for additional waitresses, bus boys, and cooks I could lead to Jesus that I forgot about finding out who the man was.

This started us training a lot of other people to do exactly the same thing with incredible results.

Every church wants revival, and yet if we want revival, we have to put our faith into action and go out and do something. We believe with our hearts and souls that if the body of Christ in every church in the world could get the idea of going out and saying, "There are two kinds of...." to everybody they meet, we would have a worldwide revival in record time, because real revival is getting the body of Christ turned on and really revved up to talk about Jesus! There's nothing that will send your spirit soaring more than to win somebody to Jesus.

In one church we were encouraging everybody to go out and say, "There are two kinds of people" and one lady realized that her mother was not saved and was in the hospital and not in good condition. She immediately left the church, went to the hospital, and said, "Mother, there are two kinds of patients in this hospital, those who are saved and those who are about to be. Which are you?" Believe it or not the mother said, "I think it's about time, and I'm about to be," and the daughter led her in a sinner's prayer. Do you have any idea what this did to the girl when her own mother repeated the sinner's prayer?

Remember, you cannot lose, because if the person is already saved, then it is exciting for them to hear about Jesus. If they are not saved, then you have the opportunity of bringing them right into the kingdom of God. That is a delight to Jesus because that was His sole purpose in coming to earth. He gave believers that assignment and responsibility. When we do it, we are mightily blessed—and so is Jesus.

I want to challenge you to use your imagination in whatever situation you find yourself.

Even a wrong telephone number can be exciting! A friend of ours answered the telephone, and obviously the person did not recognize her voice, so he said, "I'm sorry. I must have dialed the wrong telephone number."

She said, "No, you got the right number even if you dialed the wrong number." Then she continued, "There are two kinds of people who think they dialed the wrong number, those who are saved and those who are about to be; which are you?"

The man said, "I guess I'm about to be because nobody ever asked me that question before." He prayed a prayer asking Jesus to come into his heart and was so grateful and thanked her over and over and over again for asking him that "two kinds of" question.

He said, "No one ever asked me if I knew Jesus before today."

We have been having incredible success with this simple little tool of winning people to Jesus. Occasionally Charles likes to say, "Those who have accepted Jesus and those who are about to." I keep saying, "Those who are saved and those who are about to be."

He likes to put the name of Jesus in front of them but I vividly remember how the word *saved* struck a knife into my heart when a girl asked me, "When were you saved?" That's why I like to use the word *saved*.

We were discussing this recently with a pastor from Colorado. I said to him, "I would like to find the man who told me about how to do this! I want to thank him because millions of people have been saved as a result of this. I can't find anyone who knows who he was because as soon as I led the waitress to Jesus, he said, 'I have another appointment, so I have to go now,' and he got up and left!"

The pastor looked very intently at us and said, "Did it ever dawn on you that was an angel bringing God's special end-time revival message? That's the reason it's been so successful, because it came straight from God!" He continued, "I would not change one word the angel said!"

Shivers went up and down my spine!

Charles and I were so astonished because neither of us had thought of this possibility. Once again I called all ten people who were at the table, and not one person knew who he was. Most of them don't even remember him being there, and none of them heard him talking except me.

We believe in our hearts and souls that the man was a special angel sent by God to bring the simple end-time revival message to the body of Christ!

The Bible says of angels, *"Are they not all ministering spirits sent forth to minister for those who will inherit salvation?"* (Heb. 1:14).

This has been successful in every nation where we have conducted the census, and this is the way it is being done today all over the world. Those few little words are anointed by God! His presence is felt every time we ask someone the question.

We had an astonishing thing happen, because by the middle of March 1998, we had a total salvation response of 16,602,374 individuals. One month later, on April 23, we broke the 25 million mark, and the grand total at that time was 25,134,187 documented salvations.

I decided to get real rambunctious and ask God to give me 30 million salvations for my birthday. If we believe that all things are possible with God, then nothing is impossible with God. Every day we excitedly counted the totals as they came in, and on May 7, the night before my birthday, we were still 145,643 short of 30 million!

We called everybody we knew who was doing the census to see if they had any new reports in, and God answered our prayer at 10:30 that night in a most incredible way! We received a fax from the coordinator in the Philippines with a part of the eastern side of Region 6 showing 173,324 new souls in the kingdom of God. God gave us not only 30 million, He gave us *"exceedingly, abundantly above all that we* [could] *ask or think"* (Eph. 3:20). It brought the incredible total on the day of my birthday to 30,027,883. Hallelujah!

I couldn't think of anything that I wanted more for my birthday than 30 million souls, and that is exactly what God did!

Everything is being accelerated so rapidly that we must all remember that we don't have time to do things the way we used to. We have used the Roman Road and other successful tools to win people to Jesus over the past years. Today there is no longer any time to use something that takes as much time as that when you are knocking on every door in the world.

The World Evangelistic Census (WEC) is moving so rapidly that it is difficult for us to keep up with it day by day. However, as of March 1, 2000, some very interesting facts have surfaced.

Salvations per Second as of March 1, 2000

243,665,046 total salvations

26 months

9,371,732.54 salvations per month

30.5 days in a month

307,269.92 salvations per day

24 hours in a day

12,802.91 salvations per hour

60 minutes in an hour

213.38 salvations per minute

60 seconds in a minute

3.56 people being born again per second for the last 26 months

Standing Shoulder to Shoulder

243,665,046 salvations x 2 feet, the normal width of a person

487,330.92 total feet

131,480,184 feet (distance around the world)

Standing shoulder to shoulder, the people saved in about 26 months would go around the world 3 and 1/3 times!

Putting a Mustard Seed Side by Side

243,665,046 salvations

0.058 of an inch—size of a mustard seed

4,132,572.67 total mustard seeds

12 inches per foot

1,177,714.39 total feet

5,280 total feet in a mile

223.05 miles putting a seed side by side

Premise: As each person accepts Jesus due to the WEC, they join the line of saved people that is circling the world. One person takes the hand of the last person in line and then reaches out for the next person to join the line. If you were to travel alongside, you would have to run, drive, or fly 9.709 miles per hour just to keep even with the evergrowing line of those being saved.

Assume: Each person takes up four feet to stand with arms reaching side to side to grasp hands with someone on either side.

3.46 persons being saved per second

4 feet to stand holding hands with the next person

14.24 feet per second

60 seconds in a minute

854.4 feet per minute

60 minutes per hour

51,264 feet per hour

5,280 feet in a mile

9.7090909 miles per hour

Note: The four-minute mile equals fifteen miles per hour.

Philippians 2:10 states that at the very mention of the name of Jesus, every knee will bow and every tongue will confess that Jesus Christ is Lord. Even the unholy spirits affecting the mouths of the "religious unsaved"—Hindus, etc.—will have to move aside for the great anointing upon that wonderful name of Jesus.

"For there is no distinction between Jew and Greek, for the same Lord over all is rich to all who call upon Him. For 'whoever calls upon the name of the LORD shall be saved'" (Rom. 10:12–13).

You will notice that verse says, *"Whoever calls upon the name of the Lord shall be saved."* Since God the Father already knows the date Jesus is coming back to earth, we believe that His enforcement of Scriptures will intensify as the day draws nearer. Because there is a premium on time, things need to get done and will get done quickly and in ways far surpassing the methods of old. The closer the return of Jesus, the less time it will take to convert someone. God has already prepared the hearts all over the world! It won't take hours of persuasion.

The Bible says, "Will a nation be born in a day?" (See Isaiah 66:8.) This is a fact, not just a question; therefore, the way to do it has to be done quickly! Since the Word of God tells us that all we have to do is call upon the name of the Lord to be saved (Rom. 10:13), we believe that you will see the Holy Spirit sweep across an entire nation. As a result, they all will suddenly raise their hands to God and cry out, "Jesus," and a whole nation will be saved in one day!

As of the writing of this book in March 2000, the figures are over 244 million documented souls saved, and it is hard to believe! That is over four percent of the population of the earth saved in about twenty-six months. That is nearly one-fourth of a billion souls saved in about twenty-six months. Watch what God will do before the return of Jesus, and be utterly astounded! Our finite minds cannot understand the acceleration of God, but we need to get our thinking established so that we can.

God will often confound and encourage you while you are obeying Him. I personally do not have dreams that are significant, but Saturday night, May 30, 1998, I had an unusual dream.

All of the salvations you hear us talk about are documented salvations where people have written their names on a slip of paper, saying, "I have accepted Jesus as my Savior and Lord."

We have six telephone lines coming into our office at the present time, but in my dream, suddenly we increased it to ten! We were all in the office early one morning when suddenly all ten lines lit up at once. Everyone in the office ran for a telephone because we had never seen ten lines light up at one time.

I answered a telephone along with everybody else, and there was a very excited person on the other end of the line, and he was saying, "We just ended the census in the country of Timbucktu, and we got 794,622 people saved!" I thought, "Wow! This is really exciting because I didn't even know we had anyone working there!" The person on the other end was so excited as he told me how they did it that I could hardly sit still in my seat. I could hardly wait to run and tell Charles about the telephone call that I had, but when I finally hung up after I got the man's name, address, and a little more information, the telephone rang again, so I had to pick it up.

In the meantime, the same thing was happening all over the office. Everyone was receiving a telephone call from some foreign country that we had probably never even heard about, and they were giving incredible reports about what was happening on the census.

My secretary, whose office is right next to mine, kept trying to run into my office, and she couldn't even get to the door because she started saying, "Somebody just called with...." She couldn't even tell me how many salvations there were because the minute one phone was hung up, it would start ringing again. We finally discovered at the end of the day that all of the telephone calls were sharing exactly the same thing. It was people all over the world calling in with incredible salvation reports.

God's Word says, *"'Not by might nor by power, but by My Spirit,' says the Lord"* (Zech. 4:6), and His Spirit is moving all over the earth. That's what excites us so, because we know that if God wasn't doing this, we certainly would be incapable of doing what is being done now.

Please let me share more of the dream.

Then I heard a tremendous roar coming down the street. Our office is on a quiet country road, and suddenly there were thousands of people coming down this narrow road! They were all shouting and yelling.

Every one of them had little pieces of white paper up in the air, which they were waving. All of these little slips of paper had salvations written down on them!

They came in the door like a storm and went completely through the entire office until every office and even our warehouse was jammed to capacity with people waving these little pieces of paper. They even got so excited that they stood on everyone's desks, trying to get to us to show us these remarkable salvations as we continued answering the telephone calls.

There wasn't room in the office for anybody or anything else when suddenly I saw through the window that there were people standing outside. The windows on the west side of our building are high off the ground, so people had to stand on somebody else's shoulders to be able to get up to the windows so that they could show us the little pieces of paper with salvations written down on them.

In the dream, everyone got so excited because everybody had the same kind of reports to make. In our spirits we felt that this was something special from God, saying, "Get ready, because this is what I'm going to do. I'm going to explode this evangelistic census. Then when it's over, Jesus will come back."

I was so excited about the dream that I could hardly wait to call our office on Monday morning to tell them what had happened. Our graphics man who has been with us for thirteen years answered the phone and said, "Frances, would you like to hear a dream I had Saturday night?" I said, "Wait until you hear the dream I had Saturday night!" I said, "Tell me yours."

He said, "I dreamed we moved our offices into a sixty-story office building, and our offices were on the top floor." He said, "I was on the sixtieth floor and was going down to the first floor, but the elevator stopped on the fifty-ninth floor. The doors opened, and that whole floor was jammed by people with handfuls of slips of paper wanting to give them to me because they were the names of people who had accepted Jesus!"

Then he said, "The elevator stopped on the fifty-eighth floor, and it was the same thing! The whole floor was jammed with people waving lots of little pieces of paper showing the number of people who had been saved."

He said, "The elevator stopped at every floor on the way down, and each floor was filled with people waving those little pieces of paper!"

If you will notice, both the dreams were basically the same, only told in a little different way. I was so excited about this that we shared it in the church where we were ministering, and the pastor of the church got up and said, "Let me share a vision God gave to me in 1984 in Louisiana." Here is his story:

> God called me in the middle of a Wednesday night about 11:30 PM, and everyone was in bed. He spoke to me audibly. At first I was a little frightened. I thought I was going crazy! I looked in the kitchen to see if somebody was playing a game with me, and there was nobody there; they were all in bed. My sons were in bed. My wife was in bed.
>
> Again the voice came and said, "Get on the floor. I want to talk to you." The Lord spoke to me audibly for some time. That happened two nights in a row. The third night He did the same thing, and then He gave me a vision. I'd never had a vision before or since like this. I have had heart visions. I have had dreams that I knew were from the Lord. I shook my head, opened my eyes,

tried to get rid of it but couldn't. He wanted to show me something.

I think I left my body, the best I can tell. I went above the earth, and I was standing in space outside of time, looking down at the earth. No time was involved.

He showed me a wave that billowed up at a certain point of the earth, and then this wave started to move! On the front side of the wave was the cutting edge where great and mighty things take place. On the back side of the wave there were millions of people getting saved. I saw that the second night.

A wave of glory went around the entire earth, and God told me to tell everybody about it. Awesome healings and miracles took place as I was watching this incredible wave of glory. People were getting legs who didn't have legs, getting hands who didn't have hands before. People preaching in barrooms and bowling alleys; people getting saved on the sidewalks; miracles happening—that's what we're talking about.

On the back edge after the wave had gone around, I saw boats lined up. That wave of glory left a huge lake. The boats were floating on that lake. The people in the boats were grabbing folks. These boats were lined up nose-to-nose, side-by-side, all the way around the earth. There was no place where there wasn't a boat. They were everywhere.

The Lord had all these people in the water, and that was His glory. Some were drowning in it because they refused help. I imagine there were people on those boats saying, "There are two kinds of people in this lake...." People were honest. People were reaching out and grabbing them by the hands, throwing them into the boats by the hair, by the face, by anything they could grab. Kids, moms, dads, teenagers—just throwing them in. These boats were full, and they weren't sitting real nice. You could see elbows, legs, bottoms, heads. They were just throwing them in.

I was serious as I could be and I said, "Lord, those boats are going to sink!" That was my first thought when I saw how full they were. I said, "Those boats are going to sink!' He said, "Son, those boats don't sink. You just keep bringing them in!" *"From now on you will catch men"* (Luke 5:10).

The wave of glory went around the entire world, and the further it got, the faster it went! Then when it reached what looked like 5 o'clock, the wave went "swish" all the way around the world. It hit where it started, and a geyser of water went up into the air, and Jesus appeared in the middle of that water spout!

In just the last week, some of the most incredible things have happened that we have ever seen. If you will notice, these two dreams and the vision are exactly the same thing— God alerting us to be ready for the end-time harvest. There is no question in our minds whatsoever that the census is the end-time harvest!

We were speaking in a church in Austin, Texas, last week where the people had said, "We want to be a part of this end-time harvest, so we want you to come down and take an offering!" Just as we got into the church building, someone ran up to us and said, "Don't go inside the church until you make this telephone call." They said it was urgent; it was critical!

Charles made the telephone call quickly to discover that a fax had just come in from India stating that there were 8,447,000 new salvations from that country. This brought the total salvations in India to 18,333,000. As if this wasn't enough, we came home and went to Mesa, Arizona, and Saturday morning we received a fax telling us that there were 132 salvations in Colombia, 3,953 salvations in Peru, and 1,887,394 salvations in the Philippines! This is acceleration if we ever saw acceleration in our lives. Then when we came home from Arizona on Sunday, there was another fax from Bhadravati, India, with 390,000 additional salvations, bringing the worldwide total at this point to 49,288,493.

What is happening today is awesome, and if we did not believe what it says in Habakkuk 1:5 we would not be able to believe these phenomenal figures. Never in the history of the world have millions come to salvation in such a short period of time, but Habakkuk 1:5 says, *"Look among the nations and watch; be utterly astounded! For I will work a work in your days which you would not believe, though it were told you."*

The *Amplified* version says, *"Look around [you, Habakkuk, replied the Lord] among the nations and see! And be astonished! Astounded! For I am putting into effect a work in your days that you would not believe it if it were told you."*

God is doing a new thing. There are certain Scriptures I am hearing over and over and over again. Does Jesus believe these Scriptures? Yes, because Jesus believes in the fulfillment of everything that happened in the Old Testament.

Isaiah 42:9 says, *"Behold, the former things have come to pass, and new things* [brand new ones] *I declare, before they spring forth I tell you of them."*

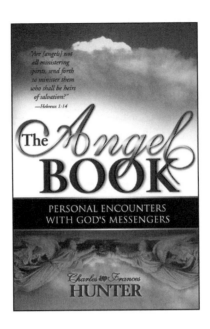

The Angel Book:
Personal Encounters with God's Messengers
Charles and Frances Hunter

Charles and Frances Hunter describe their own personal
encounters with angels and what the Bible tells us about these
messengers of God. They report on the different kinds of angels
and their roles, how God's messengers can impact your life, and
how to experience the presence of God. From these stirring
accounts, you will discover that angels are sent by God to
be your powerful protectors and helpers.

ISBN: 0-88368-598-1 • Trade • 216 pages

W

WHITAKER
HOUSE

proclaiming the power of the Gospel through the written word
visit our website at www.whitakerhouse.com

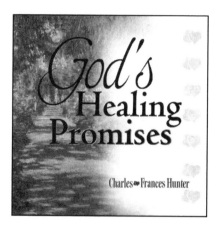

God's Healing Promises
Charles and Frances Hunter

There is healing in God's words because they are
words of promise. Here are God's life-giving words,
interspersed with faith-affirming testimonies, to bring
you health and restoration. Saturate yourself in these
expressions of healing, apply them to yourself,
and receive the promise of His Word.

ISBN: 0-88368-630-9 • 6″ x 6″ Gift Book • 176 pages

Ⅲ
WHITAKER
HOUSE

proclaiming the power of the Gospel through the written word
visit our website at www.whitakerhouse.com

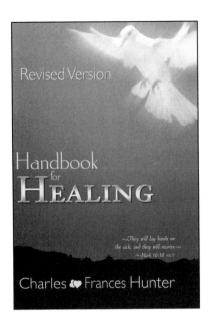

Handbook for Healing
Revised Version
Charles and Frances Hunter

In this recently updated and expanded edition, Charles and Frances Hunter present the keys to healing that they have found in the Bible and through the innovations of medical science. Written as a complement to the their best-selling *How to Heal the Sick,* this book is essential for your library—and your ministry. Discover that God can use you to bring healing and help to family, friends, and everyone you come in contact with. No longer will you have to stand by, helpless, when people are hurting!

ISBN: 0-88368-705-4 • Trade • 224 pages

ɰ
WHITAKER
HOUSE

proclaiming the power of the Gospel through the written word
visit our website at www.whitakerhouse.com

How to Heal the Sick
Charles and Frances Hunter

A loved one is sick…your friend was just in an accident…a family member is facing an emotional crisis. Have you ever desperately longed to reach out your hand and bring healing to these needs? At times our hearts ache with the desire to help, but either we don't know how or we are afraid and stop short. The truth is that, as a Christian, the Holy Spirit within you is ready to heal the sick! Charles and Frances Hunter present solid, biblically based methods of healing that can bring not only physical health, but also spiritual wholeness and the abundant life to you, your family, and everyone around you.

ISBN: 0-88368-600-7 • Trade • 224 pages

WU
WHITAKER
HOUSE

proclaiming the power of the Gospel through the written word
visit our website at www.whitakerhouse.com

I Promise...Love, God
Charles and Frances Hunter

God is sending you a message—a message of His love for you. He's been trying to get your attention, to let you know that a thrilling life awaits you. Have you been ignoring His efforts to contact you? He wants to tell you about all His promises. He wants you to understand that the promises in His Word are true and that they're for you. In these pages, you'll find promises from every book in the Bible, compiled by best-selling authors Charles and Frances Hunter. Now that God has gotten your attention, you'll be on the road to never missing Him again!

ISBN: 0-88368-668-6 • 7″ x 8″ Gift Book • 336 pages

WHITAKER HOUSE

proclaiming the power of the Gospel through the written word
visit our website at www.whitakerhouse.com